Reacting to Life's Situations

Reacting to Life's Situations

As Illustrated by Bible Personalities

MARLIN MULL

RESOURCE *Publications* · Eugene, Oregon

REACTING TO LIFE'S SITUATIONS
As Illustrated by Bible Personalities

Resource Publications
An Imprint of Wipf and Stock Publishers
199 W. 8th Ave., Suite 3
Eugene, OR 97401

www.wipfandstock.com

PAPERBACK ISBN: 978-1-6667-4607-5
HARDCOVER ISBN: 978-1-6667-4608-2
EBOOK ISBN: 978-1-6667-4609-9

08/04/22

"In this delightful book, Marlin Mull shows us that the Bible provides a relevant response to our challenging situations. Through his extraordinary gift of storytelling, Mull allows biblical characters to speak for themselves about their situations and then brings it home to us in a personal and compelling way."

—**MARK O. WILSON**, Southern Wesleyan University

"Dr. Marlin Mull is insightful, perceptive, and highly practical. He has learned much in dealing with life's situations and shares valuable lessons in these pages. Drawing upon both life and biblical stories, he helps his readers identify productive principles for personal decision-making and daily living."

—**HOWARD B. CASTLE**, former director of estate planning, the Wesleyan Church World Headquarters

"The author and his writing are practical and to the point. This book is full of wisdom drawn from biblical characters and events. . . . Read this and find how best to react when life throws challenging situations and circumstances your way."

—**PATRICK STYERS**, district superintendent, Florida District, the Wesleyan Church

"Dr. Mull has lived a life compelled by connecting people to God so they can discover the fullest meaning of life. This book is a creative way to help those already connected and those still searching to see these opportunities for wholeness from a fresh point of view."

—**JERRY LUMSTON**, district superintendent, NC West District, the Wesleyan Church

"*Reacting to Life's Situations* is such a fun and inspirational read! Marlin Mull takes a few well-known Bible characters and gives them nicknames, allowing them to tell their 'story' in a new way with new insights. . . . Open your heart to the messages you receive in reading this intriguing book."

—**NANCY HEER**, retired general director, Wesleyan Women

Contents

Introduction

EVERY DAY WE REACT to life, either positively or negatively. And our response can often fall between what is best and not desirable. We may have to choose what we believe to be the lesser of two evils. Even not reacting outwardly is still reacting, for even that response is an inward reaction. Daily we react. No choice as to whether or not we react. Life forces us to reply.

A review of some people's reactions to their life situations as recorded in the Bible allows us to observe their responses. And the lessons we can learn from their experiences can, if we allow them, assist us in our daily reactions to life's situations.

The Bible is difficult to ignore even when it does not specifically provide an answer to a life question or situation. Sometimes readers will scoff and deny the Bible's relevance. Yet various life principles are given from the outset.

Whether through Moses or David in the Old Testament, or others like Matthew, Mark, Luke, John, and Paul in the New Testament, the Bible's words offer wisdom and guidance as we respond to our personal life situations.

Over the centuries, though always challenged, the Bible continues to capture the minds and wills of its readers as they live out its principles. In the affirming words of Jesus in Matt 24:35, *"Sky and earth will wear out; but my words won't wear out."*

The Bible can, if followed, uniquely guide us through a fast changing world of increasing human knowledge. The Bible comes down through the ages as the unparalleled book with no equals. Passing through many hands, in different languages and translations, it remains the most-read book of all time.

The Bible answers life's gigantic questions with assurance. "Where did I come from?" "Who am I?" "Where am I going?" "Is there life after death?"

Just a strong suggestion: read it and apply it. Discover the relevance the Holy Bible can have in your reactions to life's situations that confront you.

Join me in the adventures of various biblical characters—with a twist. In these personal story accounts of Bible personalities, as they might possibly tell it, the attempts strive to be accurate to the Scripture's character. With the additional use of imagination, secular history, and the customs of biblical times, I try to fill in some possible scenarios relating to the person being presented that make their example applicable to your life and mine.

It is my prayer that these thoughts will help prepare you for a fulfilling life in Jesus Christ by reacting to and accepting his call to follow him, the number one person and personality of the Bible and history.

—Dr. Marlin Mull

Joseph the *Innocent* Bystander

The birth of Jesus took place like this. His mother, Mary, was engaged to be married to Joseph. Before they came to the marriage bed, Joseph discovered she was pregnant. (It was by the Holy Spirit, but he didn't know that.) 19 Joseph, chagrined but noble, determined to take care of things quietly so Mary would not be disgraced.

20 While he was trying to figure a way out, he had a dream. God's angel spoke in the dream: "Joseph, son of David, don't hesitate to get married. Mary's pregnancy is Spirit-conceived. God's Holy Spirit has made her pregnant. 21 She will bring a son to birth, and when she does, you, Joseph, will name him Jesus—'God saves'—because he will save his people from their sins." 22 This would bring the prophet's embryonic sermon to full term:

> *23 Watch for this—a virgin will get pregnant and bear a son;*
> *They will name him Emmanuel (Hebrew for "God is with us").*

24 Then Joseph woke up. He did exactly what God's angel commanded in the dream: He married Mary. 25 But he did not consummate the marriage until she had the baby. He named the baby Jesus.

MATTHEW 1:18–25

I WANT TO SHARE Joseph's story for him, the husband of the Virgin Mary, as I imagine it might have happened, because the Bible does not record any words spoken by him. Too often we equate silence with weakness. Joseph, the silent type, revealed the strength of his character by his actions.

Joseph means "dreamer." The dreamer dreamed, fulfilling his name. The young man anticipated the day when he would marry the girl of his dreams. Joseph remembered being aware of Mary several years before thinking of marriage. Younger than Joseph by several years, the teenager possessed an unusual maturity that captured his heart. You might call it love at first sight. Their parents also sensed their attraction toward one another.

Parents arranged marriages in those days, so Joseph was thrilled when his father began negotiations with Mary's father to prepare for their wedding even though it would occur several years in the future.

Joseph recalled the arrangements before the public officials of Nazareth who witnessed the written agreement of marriage between Joseph's and Mary's families for their children. The agreement laid out in detail the amount of dowry to be paid over the years to Mary's father and family for Joseph to be her husband in the future. They became legally engaged. The legal engagement agreement so bound Joseph and Mary together that it could not be broken except by a process ending with a paper of divorce. An engagement meant real commitment. Both Joseph and Mary looked forward to making that commitment a reality when they would be married in a few years.

Joseph and Mary often walked home from the synagogue together, as they held hands, discussing their future wedding and plans for a home of their own. In Joseph's mind, Mary exhibited purity of love and devotion to God and to him.

In the time that passed until Joseph could wed Mary, her dowry was paid regularly to her parents. It involved woodworking projects that he and his father worked on together. His labor of love and anticipation of marriage to Mary made the work seem as nothing. Joseph and Mary would be husband and wife soon.

Their heritage in the tribe of Judah reached back to King David. Mary traced her ancestry back to King David and Bathsheba's son Nathan. Joseph knew he was descended from King David through David and Bathsheba's son King Solomon. Royalty flowed through their veins.

Nathan the prophet spoke for the Lord to King David in 2 Samuel 7:16, *"Your family and your kingdom are permanently secured. I'm keeping my eye on them! And your royal throne will always be there, rock solid."*

More importantly, both Joseph and Mary devotedly worshiped the Lord God Jehovah faithfully. They attended and performed, when possible, all the required services and rituals given by Jehovah to Moses for the nation of Israel. In their hearts they both lived holy and pure lives before God and man. Both were exceptional young people and very much in love.

Then one day just before their marriage date, Mary approached Joseph with a different look on her face, reflecting that something was definitely not right. She spoke hesitantly to Joseph: "Joseph, I'm with child." He replied, "Surely you are not serious. How can it be?"

Mary explained how the angel Gabriel visited her and told her she would be with child when the Holy Spirit came upon her, yet she would remain a virgin.

Joseph's dream world vanished. Who did this to his beloved Mary? Who did this to his pure and innocent beloved? Who could have taken advantage of her? The unthinkable, the unimaginable, the unwelcome happened—WITH CHILD! Therefore, Joseph doubted and found Mary's story unbelievable!

How would Joseph react? His fiancée expected a baby, and he knew someone else had to be the father!

How Mary approached Joseph on the subject, we do not know. However it was, she explained it, and he rejected it. The explanation of an angel's announcement did not satisfy him. And Joseph experienced painful consternation and dismay.

Her explanation could be considered profane. Mary claims God did this to her! What an absurd justification for her sin.

His reasonable conclusion makes perfect sense from a human perspective. An unwelcome nightmare is definitely not a good thing, nor is the excruciating emotional pain that follows and strikes hard. The pain of a rejected, broken heart wouldn't go away. The unbelievable had happened. All of life's dreams for him and Mary vanished with just two words, "with child"!

Before we harshly judge Joseph, please remember, we wouldn't have believed Mary either! The perplexing problem of doubt calls on all of us in trying situations. The human side meets with doubt, but how do we handle it? Joseph the innocent bystander deals with this doubt and rightfully so.

For a few moments, let's reflect realistically about his possible reactions and the turmoil in his mind.

∼

I have no idea what I am going to do. I know I need to make the right decision, because despite the situation, I still love Mary. Several options present themselves that I can possibly pursue to get us out of or at least improve this situation. After reviewing the options stated in the Scriptures, I am left with a feeling of complete despair. I want to do the right thing according to the Scriptures.

Mary's father already made up his mind that he would send her off to a relative to have the child and avoid shaming himself and the family.

A scripturally sound choice could be to have her stoned for adultery, violating our engagement agreement. No! I love her too much to have her put to death.

Another option would be a divorce from our engagement. So this I intend to do as the Bible records in Matt 1:1: *"Joseph, chagrined but noble, determined to take care of things quietly so Mary would not be disgraced."*

With a broken heart and feelings of betrayal, my heart and head do not want to embarrass Mary further. I'll handle the divorce quickly and quietly.

People will talk. From now on, the conversations will be about my problem with Mary. I will be the talk of Nazareth. Even my friends might distance themselves with chuckles and snide comments. The scent of scandal will leave people wondering about what really happened. I will deny being the father, but who will believe me?

I've made my decision. I will divorce Mary even though we never lived together as husband and wife. That's the truth, God being my witness.

That night I dropped off into a fitful sleep and began to dream. God spoke to me in a dream and gave me directions. I needed a word from the Lord. He whispered to me what to do in a dream.

> *"Joseph, son of David, don't hesitate to get married. Mary's pregnancy is Spirit-conceived. God's Holy Spirit has made her pregnant. 21 She will bring a son to birth, and when she does, you, Joseph, will name him Jesus—'God saves'— because he will save his people from their sins." 22 This would bring the prophet's embryonic sermon to full term: 23 Watch for this—a virgin will get pregnant and bear a son; They will name him Emmanuel (Hebrew for "God is with us").* (Matt 1:20b–23)

Morning came. And with the sunlight of a new day I at first wondered whether I could believe this dream. Last night my mother gave me an extra piece of dessert. Could my overeating have caused the dream?

But I believed. What a dream! An astronomically inconceivable vision came to my mind.

Mary's child is conceived by the Holy Spirit. She did remain true to me. Mary still loves me and wants me to be her husband. What an incredible and unbelievable message. So I'll obey God. I'll do what the angel of the Lord said. I'll marry Mary now. As crazy as it all may sound, as illegitimate as it looks, God validates this pregnancy.

From this moment on, I became more than an innocent bystander. I had a role to fulfill. This baby required me to dutifully perform as a father.

Let me share some of the things assigned to me as the earthly father who adopted Jesus as my own son.

I protected him from others who would call him derogatory words as a child born out of wedlock. I defended his right as my son without any sigma being attached to the relationship.

From my mind and with heart and hands, I taught and shared with Jesus the carpenter's trade as my father taught me. Jesus, my son, is God and omniscient. He did not need any instruction from me, but allowed me, Joseph, to fulfill the role of an earthly father working with the heavenly God in the plan of salvation.

Often when Jesus spoke to the multitudes, he used illustrations from the carpenter's shop. He spoke about his yoke being easy. Jesus described and contrasted houses being either built on sand or rock to illustrate life. Jesus remembered that when we finished a day's work in our shop, we would fold up our towels and lay them on the workbench to signify being through for the day. I died several years before Jesus was crucified, but on resurrection morning the carpenter also arose. Before Jesus left the tomb, he took the burial cloth and folded it by itself to signify that his work was completed. Salvation's plan was completed and finished forever.

Joseph's Reactions

When dreams burst like soap bubbles, how do we gather up the residue? And when life as expected becomes the unexpected, what do we expect from God?

The Bible highly commends Joseph using the descriptive word "righteous" with its rich spiritual meaning of uprightness, righteousness, integrity, and morality.

I believe Joseph first prayed to Jehovah. Then he studied the Scriptures. God then revealed the steps for Joseph to take in a dream.

And if we closely follow Joseph's reactions patiently, I believe God will show in his perfect time the response we should give.

Joseph clearly had a lasting influence on the life of Jesus and others.

Did Joseph ever see or hear Jesus perform miracles or preach to the multitudes? Doubtful!

Did Joseph see his resurrected son on earth? No!

Did Joseph gather in the Upper Room with the disciples on the Day of Pentecost when the Holy Spirit came on the birthday of the church? No!

Did Joseph see his son ascend into heaven? No!

Did Joseph ever know that his and Mary's son James became the head of the church? No!

Did Joseph realize that James and Jude, his and Mary's sons, would write books that would be in the Bible? No!

Joseph lived such a life that Jesus Christ the Son of God obeyed him as a child growing up. It is a daring theological thought that God allowed himself to be under man's jurisdiction.

We do not worship a man like Joseph, but we do hope there will be more like him.

If we are to react to life's difficult situations properly, we need to be in a right relationship with God through Jesus Christ that can identify us as "righteous" like Joseph. Therefore, "Be righteous."

An Illustration from Personal Experience

Let me share about two of many righteous men and women I knew as a pastor. The first part of this accounting of how they became Christians happened before I knew them.

Alvin and Marie's marriage was blessed with two children, both girls. Jesus Christ and church were not a part of their lives, as their successful restaurant was open seven days a week for twelve to fourteen hours a day. They were not against Christianity, but they primarily deemed it unnecessary. But something seemingly insignificant at that time changed and challenged their entire perception of how to live.

A children's Sunday school teacher put forth a special effort to visit the family and offered to take the two children to Sunday school every week and bring them home. Alvin and Marie agreed, as their girls wanted to go and enjoyed Sunday school and church. This arrangement went on for several months until there was a special program at the church featuring the girls as a part of it. Their parents went and also enjoyed the church and its services.

After a few months of attending the church, Alvin and Marie both dedicated their lives to Jesus Christ and the church that Jesus died to establish. Alvin in a few years became a lay leader serving on the church governing body, and Marie became the church treasurer. Both could accurately be described as righteous people.

One thing in particular demonstrated the righteousness of Alvin and Marie's lives. Alvin and Marie sold their restaurant and started another business. Their source of income came from digging holes for septic tanks in the mountains of North Carolina. Their clients were located sometimes fifty to sixty miles away, often requiring one to two hours of travel to reach their destination. In the Blue Ridge mountain area where they lived, the ground often froze, making it impossible for Alvin to work daily during the winter months of December through March. Their main source of income came from about eight months out of the year. The other four months he did small jobs and repaired and kept his machines in good condition.

However, even in his busiest months after working about twelve-hour days, when it came time for the Wednesday prayer and Bible study service at 7:00 p.m., he would be there. If his job took him one or two hours away from home, he would stop in the afternoon to be in church that night. His dedication cost him a lot of income during his busiest and most profitable time. Alvin lived a righteous life by example. He never talked about his sacrifice to attend church, as like Joseph he was a man of few words. Alvin's personal convictions about Christianity may not be for others and their church attendance, but his actions spoke volumes of testimony to his personal conviction of faithfulness to Christ and his church.

In reacting to whatever life situation you confront, one question to always keep in mind is whether or not you are following your personal, God-given convictions. They may not be required of others, but God requires them of you for your personal spiritual benefit. As best you know, stay in the center of God's will for your life.

Sam, a Shepherd

There were sheepherders camping in the neighborhood. They had set night watches over their sheep. 9 Suddenly, God's angel stood among them and God's glory blazed around them. They were terrified. 10 The angel said, "Don't be afraid. I'm here to announce a great and joyful event that is meant for everybody, worldwide: 11 A Savior has just been born in David's town, a Savior who is Messiah and Master. 12 This is what you're to look for: a baby wrapped in a blanket and lying in a manger."

13 At once the angel was joined by a huge angelic choir singing God's praises:

14 Glory to God in the heavenly heights,
Peace to all men and women on earth who please him.

15 As the angel choir withdrew into heaven, the sheepherders talked it over. "Let's get over to Bethlehem as fast as we can and see for ourselves what God has revealed to us." 16 They left, running, and found Mary and Joseph, and the baby lying in the manger. 17 Seeing was believing. They told everyone they met what the angels had said about this child. 18 All who heard the sheepherders were impressed.

19 Mary kept all these things to herself, holding them dear, deep within herself. 20 The sheepherders returned and let loose, glorifying

and praising God for everything they had heard and seen. It turned out exactly the way they'd been told!

LUKE 2:8–20

THREE PHRASES OFTEN REPEATED seem to sum up thoughts about Christmas these days: "Peace on Earth," "Goodwill to Men," and "Batteries not included." Let's consider peace on earth primarily today.

Let me introduce myself. Call me Sam the shepherd. Centuries ago I tended sheep in the land of Palestine for a living and even today am uncomfortable sharing my life's story with others. Give me the open fields. Having never received a formal education, my father trained me in the only skill he knew—shepherding. And I'm not a theologian either. My parents told me the stories of our forefathers—those great men and women of faith like Abraham, Moses, David, and Esther. We sang the psalms from memory like all good Hebrews and, when allowed, visited the synagogue to hear the rabbi teach. We didn't mingle a lot with other people. Being a shepherd didn't place you very high on the social ladder of life, rather closer to the bottom. Hard and monotonous work, you spent most of your time outdoors, exposed to the elements. In your modern world, you fence in pastures and build elaborate barns to care for your livestock. But we shepherds operated differently. Our sheep grazed in the open countryside. We led them to green pastures to eat and still waters to drink, walking every step of the way. No trucks or animal carriers were available for our use like you have now.

Predators constantly threatened. A shepherd's job involved protecting his flock from snakes, bears, wolves, and the occasional marauding lion. On a few occasions, I almost lost my life protecting my sheep.

Nobody ever said it, but we could always tell that most folks didn't want us around. The reason—the way we looked and smelled. If you live and work outside with livestock, very little time remains to trim your beard, take a bath, and clean your clothes. Spending most of your life with sheep, you begin to smell like them. Sheep are filthy animals. A sheep in the field is as nasty as a hog. The white sheep wool you see ready for use goes through a thorough cleansing process. You can imagine the reaction of people in town when shepherds would stop in for supplies. They'd take our money, but we could tell they wanted us to leave quickly.

People generally mistrusted shepherds. Perhaps it was because of our nomadic lifestyle, moving from place to place. If an item went missing, the shepherd automatically became the most likely suspect. Unfair! Maybe some dishonest men came from my trade, but isn't that the case in all professions? For some reason a large number of the people classified us all as scoundrels. Even the judges believed this. They wouldn't readily allow the testimony of a shepherd in any court case.

The attitude of the religious leaders toward us hurt and angered me the most. Being part of a special group of shepherds who raised the lambs used for sacrifice in the temple at Jerusalem, we worked diligently raising those sheep. We picked out the best male lambs for the priests, without spots or blemishes. We never pawned off blind or crippled sheep. We believed that God deserved the best sheep for sacrifices made to him as we worshiped.

Our efforts went unrecognized by the priests. In fact, they often sneered at us when we brought the lambs. The priests paid us and then the temple guards drove us out as quickly as possible. I guess they didn't want grimy shepherds cluttering up the place.

The religious people looked down on us because we didn't attend the services and feasts consistently. We wanted to, but we couldn't. Shepherding was a 24/7 job. They never saw the connection. We could present them perfect lambs to sacrifice, but only because we worked so hard at our jobs. Because we worked so hard, we couldn't possibly be present at all the religious celebrations. They considered us ceremonially unclean. The Pharisees set up elaborate cleansing rituals for those who wanted to be admitted to participate in temple worship. We could never be clean enough for them.

The priests and the scribes and the Pharisees looked down on us. Those whom others considered the righteous people completely despised us. I began to wonder if perhaps God did too.

That idea that God considered us unworthy of his love forever vanished from my mind the night the angel appeared. I know this will sound weird, but it really happened. I hope that, unlike my countrymen, you will trust in the testimony I'm about to share.

It happened late one night in early winter. I remember the season well, because that's when the rains come to our land. The barren fields of Judea become lush with vegetation for a few weeks during December and January. Many of the neighboring shepherds gathered their sheep together in a meadow just outside of Bethlehem. We assembled them into one big flock for protection and so we could enjoy one another's company. Some of the men slept while others told stories, or played their flutes and lyres.

Suddenly a strange silence fell over the men and animals. Those asleep simultaneously awakened from their sleep. In an instant an enormous humanlike figure materialized near the sheep. His clothes beamed a brilliant white, like snow, except brighter. Every one of us left our post to get a better look at our strange visitor. We carried our clubs and slings and swords, just in case he wanted to fight. The sheep just lay there, calm and at rest.

It's difficult for me to describe what happened next, even today. As I and the other shepherds approached the man in white, no ordinary human being, we shook with fear. Before any of us could reach our dazzling visitor, something like a bright light shone all around us. It did not blind our eyes. A pure and intense light, it penetrated my body to the very depths of my soul. Overwhelmed by the power of this light, I sensed a unique presence. In my spirit I knew this had to be the radiant glory of God that appeared to us. The fire of his presence presented itself as I'd heard about it in the ancient Hebrew scrolls.

Imagine my experience. Those who stand in the presence of the Lord God Jehovah understand his overwhelming holiness. Like Isaiah the prophet, in those moments I recognized my own filthiness. It reached beyond the dirt on my clothes, manure on my sandals, and sweat stains on my tunic. It reached my soul.

As a sinner I stood in the presence of a holy, righteous, utterly pure God. My first impulse prompted me to run and hide. But where could I flee from this heavenly scene? Yet, despite this wonderful, yet fearsome revelation, underneath it all I could feel the presence of eternal love and acceptance. I fell to my knees and then on my face.

> The angel said, "Don't be afraid. I'm here to announce a great and joyful event that is meant for everybody, world-wide: 11 A Savior has just been born in David's town, a Savior who is Messiah and Master. 12 This is what you're to look for: a baby wrapped in a blanket and lying in a manger." (Luke 2:10–12)

A warm peace filled my heart. God's message for me and for the whole world revealed not judgment but good news.

After four hundred years of silence and our Jewish people waiting for this moment, God spoke. Generations lived and died looking forward to the coming of this Deliverer. Can you believe it? God made his announcement to us—shepherds in the field. That didn't make sense. I, at that time, concluded that the religious leaders in Jerusalem must have already known and celebrated the arrival of our Savior.

Nothing unusual is connected with the fact that all good mothers wrapped their babies in cloths in those days. This kept the newborn warm and protected their limbs from injury. The snug wrap of the cloth strips made the babies feel secure.

The second part of the sign puzzled me. The messiah lies in a manger? God's anointed Savior sleeps on a bed of hay in a manger where horses and cows eat? I didn't understand, but I took him at his word.

As if my mind weren't spinning already, suddenly, as far as the eye could see, a vast multitude of angels appeared. It is kind of misleading to say they appeared. My eyes suddenly gained the ability to see them. Hundreds of them, brilliant like lightning and in various forms, dazzled the sky. With one voice they cried out:

Glory to God in the heavenly heights,
Peace to all men and women on earth who please him.
(Luke 2:14)

I could have gazed at them all night, but just as quickly, they disappeared from my sight.

At sunrise we finally came to our senses after a night without sleep. Almost immediately we agreed that we'd go find this Christ child.

Several of us started to go when the voice of reason rang out from one of the shepherds. He simply asked, "What about the sheep?" We puzzled over this for a moment, but then one of the older shepherds came up with the solution. He reminded us that if God took the time to announce this glorious event, surely he'd watch out for our sheep so that we could see the messiah. Unbelievably, some of the shepherds, like people today, remained more concerned over their sheep than meeting the Savior. A handful decided to stay. To my knowledge they never even attempted to see the child. They seemed only affected by the angels and their message as if it all happened as a dream in the night.

Those of us who made the journey to Bethlehem that morning found everything just as the messenger had said. The baby, the Christ child, slept peacefully in the manger, wrapped up snug and warm. The new mother, who couldn't have been more than sixteen, told me the baby's name was Jesus. A common name, but it means "God saves."

It perplexed me to learn that none of the religious leaders came to see the baby with Jerusalem only six miles away. Not one Jewish leader welcomed him. Did God not reveal this event to our religious leaders?

We huddled around the baby for just a little while. When it became clear that child and mother wanted to rest and sleep, we returned to our sheep.

In one night everything changed. Faith replaced my doubts. Joy replaced my frustrations. I returned to my labor as a shepherd with a peace that God loved me, a lowly shepherd. Call me "Sam, the shepherd saved by grace."

Even after all these years, many "why" questions still surface in my mind. Why did God reveal himself to me? Why did he announce the birth of his Son to a band of mainly socially unacceptable shepherds and not to the religious elite? Why did the manger provide a birth place for Christ instead of a palace like the son of a king? Why did Mary give birth to the Savior in a little town like Bethlehem and not in the holy city, Jerusalem? Why did God choose the Jewish people for the lineage of his Son? The Romans possessed more military might. The Greeks expressed more wisdom. The Egyptians exhibited more artistic values.

The only answer I could come up with to the many questions surrounding Christ's birth is that God reveals himself to those humble enough to receive him. Something those angels said sticks out in my mind. They chanted: "*Glory to God in the heavenly heights, Peace to all men and women on earth who please him.*" The angels promised peace with the birth of that child, but not the kind of peace that means cessation from war and conflict. If that were the case, then God failed miserably and history bears it out.

No, the kind of peace that the angels talked about meant a peace with God, a forgiveness resulting in a right relationship with the Almighty they proclaimed. Part of the promise includes peace within us. A peace within witnesses no matter what dark valleys we may walk through. God, like a shepherd, leads his sheep. He's there even when we can't see him, and he's leading us in the path of his purpose. That's real peace and it comes to those whom God favors. He favors those who are humble enough to receive him.

~

The angels' song gives us the hope of peace for the future. Anxiety about the future robs the peace and tranquility of today. Listen and see if these thoughts sound familiar: What if my child dies? What if my spouse dies? What if I lose my pension? What if I lose my health? What if the unspeakable tragedy that happened to our friends happens to us? Truth! Any of those things could happen to any of us. However, dwelling on our worst fears does nothing to prevent them. It robs us of our sleep, our health, our joy, and our peace of mind today.

In many ways, the world didn't dramatically change outwardly after Jesus' birth. Tragedy swiftly came. King Herod ordered the murder of many baby boys because of his own paranoia when he found out about the baby the wise men called the "King of the Jews." The authorities, both religious and governmental, publicly humiliated, beat, and executed Jesus for daring to share the audacious message that he provided a way for you and me to live at peace with God.

History reveals that from the time of Jesus' birth until today, only a few days passed on this planet without a war raging someplace. Human cruelty and a lack of regard for the sanctity of life define humanity. Human nature does not change unless Christ intervenes. Even in this century, places on this earth lie overwhelmed with poverty and injustice that defy description. Dictators and evil regimes stop at nothing to accumulate power and wealth. So it has been and so it will be.

Tragedy will come to us. But one thing will not change. The Savior the angels proclaimed that night still lives and brings peace to his followers today. The angels still proclaim their message and did not go back to just polishing their halos.

If you could receive a televised glimpse of heaven today, you would hear the angels proclaiming, "*Glory to God in the heavenly heights. Peace to all men and women on earth who please him.*"

Hundreds of years before Jesus' birth, the prophet Isaiah proclaimed peace with a prediction from the Lord: "*For a child has been born—for us! the gift of a son—for us! He'll take over the running of the world. His names will be: Amazing Counselor, Strong God, Eternal Father, Prince of Wholeness*" (Isa 9:6).

Inner peace can be found no matter what the circumstances. When your soul finds peace with God and rests in it, you have the capacity to endure, though sometimes extremely difficult, any crisis, any tragedy, and any misfortune. Let's go back to Sam the shepherd for a moment.

I'm no theologian. I'm uneducated. In the eyes of the world I'm nobody at all. But God loves you and I as somebody. When he saw fit to send his one and only Son to earth, he announced it to me, a shepherd. I'm living proof that you don't have to be special by others' standards for God to reveal himself. You just have to be humble enough to receive him.

Receive Jesus Christ as your personal Savior and you will know and daily experience an inner peace that makes life worth living.

Sam's Reactions

He obeyed God. Remember that your earthly standing does not change your standing with the Lord as a valuable person in his sight.

Obey God, if called, regardless of other factors like talents, training, and imposed social standards that may be thought lacking by some.

An Illustration from Personal Experience

Let me share an unusual true story and how the person reacted.

Transport your thinking with me back to the early 1900s. E. W. Black, a married young man with a growing family, had five children to care for. Since he was an hourly employee, his family struggled to barely afford the necessities of life, like food, clothing, and housing. In addition, his education was limited to two or three years of grammar school, and he had a lifelong speech impediment. E. W. Black stuttered. With a large family, being barely able to read, and having physical difficulties, we could honestly ask ourselves what limited opportunities were available for him in his life. The answer will surprise you.

After accepting Christ as his personal savior in a small church, he believed the Lord had called him to be a minister of the gospel. What should he do?

E. W. fervently began to read two books—the Bible and a dictionary. Those two books provided him a basic education, which he used effectively. If you digest and study the Bible and a dictionary, you will have a lot of knowledge about life. But he still stuttered. Was he really called to be a minister? Let his ministry record speak for him.

Whenever he preached, he might stutter when talking with someone before the service, but as soon as he began to lead the worship service with announcements, greetings, and prayer, there was no stuttering. When preaching, he became an eloquent speaker without stuttering. But as soon as the service was over and he began to greet people, the slight stuttering returned.

Over more than a thirty-year period of ministry, he became well known in his denomination, speaking at numerous large gatherings and always being an outstanding pastor of growing churches in North America.

His particular denomination, the Wesleyan Methodist Church, consisted at that time of around one thousand churches in North America and more overseas. The denomination supported three colleges and one Bible school. The largest of the three colleges, Houghton College in Houghton, New York, at that time in the 1930s had an average annual enrollment of more than one thousand and was recognized as one of the leading colleges in America. In 1937 the Houghton college church needed a pastor. They called a pastor who by now had written several books, preached at various denominational gatherings, lacked formal educational degrees, and carried a physical speech impediment when not in the pulpit. He served there for five years until health reasons caused him to retire in 1942.

So, if you judge your life by human standards (and they do have a place), do not be discouraged if called by the Lord to do what seems almost totally impossible. React to the Lord's call and he will lead you one step at a time.

Sonny's Story

11 Then he [Jesus] said, "There was once a man who had two sons. 12 The younger said to his father, 'Father, I want right now what's coming to me.'

"So the father divided the property between them. 13 It wasn't long before the younger son packed his bags and left for a distant country. There, undisciplined and dissipated, he wasted everything he had. 14 After he had gone through all his money, there was a bad famine all through that country and he began to hurt. 15 He signed on with a citizen there who assigned him to his fields to slop the pigs. 16 He was so hungry he would have eaten the corncobs in the pig slop, but no one would give him any.

17 "That brought him to his senses. He said, 'All those farmhands working for my father sit down to three meals a day, and here I am starving to death. 18 I'm going back to my father. I'll say to him, Father, I've sinned against God, I've sinned before you; 19 I don't deserve to be called your son. Take me on as a hired hand.' 20 He got right up and went home to his father.

"When he was still a long way off, his father saw him. His heart pounding, he ran out, embraced him, and kissed him. 21 The son started his speech: 'Father, I've sinned against God, I've sinned before you; I don't deserve to be called your son ever again.'

22 "But the father wasn't listening. He was calling to the servants, 'Quick. Bring a clean set of clothes and dress him. Put the family ring

on his finger and sandals on his feet. 23 Then get a grain-fed heifer and roast it. We're going to feast! We're going to have a wonderful time! 24 My son is here—given up for dead and now alive! Given up for lost and now found!' And they began to have a wonderful time.

LUKE 15:11–24

YOU JUST READ MY story as Jesus told it and as the Gospel of Luke recorded it in the Bible. Let me tell you some additional details about my life two millennia later.

Everyone called me Sonny, a name I did not particularly like, but I had no choice in the matter. I lived on a large farm with my parents, an older brother, and many servants.

I tried to love my brother, yet his superior attitude toward me day after day soon wore thin. Working sunup to sundown mainly hearing criticism from my brother was infuriating! Time to leave!

We were two brothers with the same mother and father, yet almost complete opposites in our views of life and what it offered. My brother lived mainly by the ancient proverb "Early to bed and early to rise makes a man healthy, wealthy, and wise." Your historians call it an old English proverb first printed in the 1400s, though my brother lived it in the first century.

I hesitate to admit it, but the only thing I would truly miss when I left home would be the daily feasts. Every day at home the dining room table was filled with an abundance of food. For breakfast there was meat, eggs, hot baked bread, and lots of rich and thick goat milk gravy. Lunch was at noon, complete with all the breads, vegetables, meats, and desserts you could ever want. In the evening when we came in from the field, another bountiful table of food greeted us. Still, my inner desire often expressed with inappropriate words and actions, won out. I longed to be a city boy, not a country bumpkin.

Life provided me at that time with many pleasures and opportunities. However, a restless nature stirred within me. Father entertained many visitors from various countries. Listening to their stories about life in the big cities stirred my already restless spirit to the breaking point. I would leave, if I could, and enjoy the benefits and good times available in a city.

I approached my father with boldness and told him I wanted my one-third inheritance as the younger son now. I told him I never intended to live in the country, farming for a living, and that it had always been my desire to live in a big city in another country.

With tears in his eyes, as I remembered our conversation, he reluctantly, with love, let me go. Father handed me the inheritance and said, "Sonny, use it wisely."

I gave him my personal family ring used over the years to charge needed items. Cutting all ties, I left home without the family ring that was equal to a modern-day credit card. Big mistake!

I looked forward to being on my own to make decisions and a name for myself in the world. The small, unknown country boy would be a big city man of fame and fortune

Arriving in the city, I found a nice place to stay. It was my intention to find work and business opportunities immediately, but I decided I needed a vacation first. Thirty days seemed long enough to have a good time and live it up. City life could now satisfy my long-pent-up desires.

Confidently I strode into the nearest bar as a stranger, but before the night ended, everyone there considered me a friend.

To quickly get acquainted, I walked up to the bar while pulling out a handful of money, placed it confidently on the bar, and in a loud voice said, "Barkeep, drinks are on me as long as the money lasts." People started crowding the bar for free drinks. Before I knew what was happening, a pretty girl was hanging on each arm while telling me how good looking and smart I was. Everyone liked me.

The partying continued for thirty days. Some of my new friends actually told me that if I ever needed any help to just call them. I really knew I should've been out looking for a job, but between staying up all night and sleeping in the next day, the days passed without any effort from me. My new friends kept telling me to enjoy myself, so I did.

Suddenly and swiftly, the money ran out. *No problem*, I thought. *My new friends said they would help me if I needed them.* So I went to several of them and asked to borrow some money until I could find work to repay them. They quickly and quietly avoided me. No help came from them. I became a stranger again and in their view just a country bumpkin they used to their advantage.

To make matters worse, a famine occurred. No work could be found by me or anyone else in the city. I happened to meet a local farmer who said he needed someone to care for his swine. He could only offer me shelter, and I could eat all that I wanted of the bean and corn cob swill fed to the hogs. Pigs! No way! My religious upbringing forbade me from eating pork or having anything to do with these filthy animals.

A few days later after being cold, hungry, and desperate, I took the job. After several long days and nights that stretched into several weeks of emotional and physical agony, a thought came to me as a last hope. Maybe, if I went home, confessed that I'd made a fool of myself, and asked for a servant's place, my father would accept me. Would he accept me on these terms? Almost immediately I remembered a story often repeated by the rabbis in the synagogue.

In that story, the younger son, like me, left home and spent all of his inheritance. When he came home with the hope of seeking his father's help, the father rejected him.

That father saw his son returning from afar and waited with his arms crossed over his chest. The son, broken down physically and mentally, now wearing only ragged clothes, begged his father to take him back. But the father looked away from him and said, "Forget it! You had your chance. You've chosen to live like a pig. Go back to your pigs. You've made your bed, now lie in it!"

Of course I knew this father would reject his son because he was a narrow-minded, strictly legalistic man, one that could even have his son stoned to death for his rebellion. In that oft-repeated story, the father turned his son away and told him he was getting exactly what he deserved according to the Old Testament idea of strict legalism. In fact, Moses strongly indicated in the book of

Deuteronomy (21:18–21) that a father could have a rebellious son stoned to death.

I felt that my father couldn't be that strict or he wouldn't have given me my inheritance so early. Would my father accept me if I returned and repented? Or would he reject me? There was only one way to find out. Anything, even death, would've been better than being cold and hungry and dying a slow death with the pigs. My only hope was to go home.

It was a long, long walk home. Months earlier I had ridden out proud and erect, sitting on a camel. My exquisite clothes at that time silently spoke of wealth and prominence. But now I slowly walked back toward home, bent over from continually looking down in shame, wearing tattered clothes, and barefooted. Also, without a decent bath, I smelled like the swine that I had lived with for several weeks. I needed help and hoped against hope that my father would help me.

Without adequate food, water, and clothes, and after walking barefooted many miles for many days, I neared home. At high noon my father's house began to appear faintly in the horizon.

Suddenly in the distance a man came running toward me. His robe was lifted up to keep from tripping as he showed his bare legs, something considered highly undignified. Men of respect never ran.

It was Father running toward me, and I immediately ran toward him with what energy I possessed. I tried to ask for forgiveness and ask for a servant's place in the home, but Father hardly listened, and though I smelled like the swine and looked like dirt, my father grabbed me, hugged and kissed me. I thought he would squeeze the life out of me. He said over and over, "Sonny, Sonny, my Sonny. I thought you might be dead, but you're alive."

I found out later that every day my father had stood at the upstairs window looking at the horizon for me to come home. Even with no shoes, shaggy hair, ragged clothes, and loss of weight, Father knew me from afar. He met me more than half way. My father really loved me, and I loved him.

Father fully accepted me back into the home. "Sonny," he said, you're my son, not a servant. Here is your son's robe." To the servants he said, *"Quick. Bring a clean set of clothes and dress him. Put the family ring on his finger and sandals on his feet. Then get a grain-fed heifer and roast it. We're going to feast!"* (Luke 15:22–23).

Father restored to me everything I had wasted away and had lost! Forever I'll carry the scars and the regrets of my sinful behavior, but Father still welcomed me home.

Then Father said, "Sonny ever since you've been gone I've had a calf set aside, feeding it only the best corn to fatten it up to produce tender steak. This was all in the hope that you would return and we could celebrate. And celebrate we will." And celebrate we did!

Sonny's Reactions

When we consider and reflect on Sonny's story, we may see at least a partial image of ourselves. His choice for life's direction that appeared wonderful at the beginning turns into despair and defeat. How did Sonny react when his dream for life turned into a nightmare? Let us think about some good choices he made in reacting to his life situation and, if needed, apply them to our lives as possible ways to react to a similar life situation.

1. Sonny acknowledged that, in this instance, he was first in the blame line. He could have criticized his parents or his brother, but he first accepted his personal responsibility.

2. He sought help from supposedly new friends in the city who disappointed him. Sonny learned that real friends will be with you in difficult times as well as good ones. Consider who your real friends are who may be willing to help when you honestly admit you made a mistake that led to your present undesired condition.

3. Sonny reacted by turning to his father for help. Fathers who love their children will help them as much as possible. Some fathers refuse to accept or assume any responsibility to help.

If you need a father figure or relatives to help you in your time of need, hopefully in your life someone filled or will fill that role. It could be a family-type relationship developed at your place of worship or your workplace. Turn to them for advice and help.

4. Sonny expressed a willingness with a humble attitude to accept with appreciation a lower status than before.

How are you reacting to your life situation today, if it is undesirable?

An Illustration from Personal Experience

This is a similar story that happened in today's world.

This young man's father and mother were both highly respected Christian ministers and leaders used by many church organizations as motivational speakers and for area crusades. One of their sons also became an outstanding minister as a founding church pastor of a congregation serving over one thousand attending weekly. But my story relates to another son.

This son, also equally gifted, studied and prepared for the ministry after responding to God's call. He served several churches with moderate success, by human standards, when compared to his brother and father. He was not a failure in any sense, other than possibly in his own mind: he did not achieve what his father and brother had.

Though in a denomination that discouraged the use of alcohol, he began to drink secretly and became an alcoholic. However, like the son in the story told by Jesus, he became desperate to change his current secret lifestyle.

In a drunken stupor late at night (for he only drank after his family had retired for the night), he called and confided in a close friend who got him some help. The family, after learning of his condition, rallied around and supported him. He recovered and once again began an effective ministry.

Reacting to Life's Situations

Therefore, if in your present life you've run out of personal resources and feel let down, get up! Leave the pen of despair and defeat and once again enjoy the riches of living for the Lord.

26

Ben the Bag Boy

12 As the day declined, the Twelve said, "Dismiss the crowd so they can go to the farms or villages around here and get a room for the night and a bite to eat. We're out in the middle of nowhere."

13 "You feed them," Jesus said.

They said, "We couldn't scrape up more than five loaves of bread and a couple of fish—unless, of course, you want us to go to town ourselves and buy food for everybody." 14 (There were more than five thousand people in the crowd.)

But he went ahead and directed his disciples, "Sit them down in groups of about fifty." 15 They did what he said, and soon had everyone seated. 16 He took the five loaves and two fish, lifted his face to heaven in prayer, blessed, broke, and gave the bread and fish to the disciples to hand out to the crowd. 17 After the people had all eaten their fill, twelve baskets of leftovers were gathered up.

LUKE 9:12–17

IN THE CITY OF Capernaum, where I played and grew up over two thousand years ago, my friends called me Ben, though my mother called me Benjamin.

My hometown on the upper northwest side of the Sea of Galilee served as a small port for fishermen. My father fished for a living, so fish was a regular part of our meals.

My mother was a stay-at-home mom known throughout the area as one of the best bread makers in the city. The aroma of her bread made every day a struggle not to sneak a few pieces when she wasn't looking. It was her bread and my father's fish that helped me to become a healthy teen when the greatest day of my life occurred. That day, forever etched in my mind, happened on a Sunday, the day following our Jewish Sabbath.

Every Sabbath, my parents took our family of four boys and two girls to the synagogue for worship. It didn't take long for me to memorize the worship psalms and sing them. We also recited many portions of Moses' laws and other requirements for Jewish boys and girls growing up in Israel. We learned quickly to keep matters of religion to ourselves because the Roman army still occupied our nation. Be faithful to God, but be unobserved.

During our Sabbath school sessions, the scribes would tell us of a future messiah coming to be our Savior. They very carefully worded their remarks so as not to anger the civil authorities, yet they challenged us in each session to keep watch because the messiah could appear at any time, and he did! But that's getting ahead of the story.

Word began to spread throughout Galilee about a miracle healer and teacher named Jesus. Some stories told about him sounded too good to be true. I was taught an old saying, "If it sounds too good to be true, then it cannot possibly be true."

On Saturday we went to the synagogue to worship, but on Sunday, after my chores at home were done, I was allowed to do other things. Most did not need my parents permission. This particular Sunday, word began to spread throughout Capernaum that Jesus and his disciples would be coming through our city that day.

I wanted to see Jesus—it would be the chance of a lifetime to see the miraculous things he was said to do. I started pleading with my parents to let me go with the gathering crowds to see this Jesus.

Finally they consented to let me go with my best buddy Tom, if I promised to be home by dark and stay out of trouble.

Dressed for the weather, I quickly left before my parents changed their minds. Tom and I were almost out of sight when I heard my mother calling out "Benjamin!" *Oh no, they must've changed their minds. There would be no outing with Tom today.* Reluctantly, I turned around with the saddest face that I could make.

"Benjamin," she said, "I almost forgot that you could be gone a long time today and wouldn't be near any markets where you could buy food if you get hungry. I packed a lunch bag for you and Tom with five fresh-baked loaves and two large, cooked fish that your father caught on Friday." I hugged her and thanked her, especially since Tom hadn't thought to bring any snacks on that day—as usual. That was so like my mother, so kind and thoughtful. But on that day it would be remembered as a special blessing, because it would happen on the day I met Jesus.

Tom and I started walking toward the center of town, where a large crowd had already gathered. I caught a glimpse of a man walking along with the large crowd following him. I can't explain it, but I knew it had to be Jesus. Something unique about his voice— the look on his face—his very presence drew all of us to him. His words captivated me along with everyone else. People reached out on all sides of him, trying to just touch Jesus for good luck. But those who did experience touching Jesus seemed changed in an instant. Miracles happened. People needed help. Jesus wanted to give it to them, but in their eagerness to receive help, they nearly smothered him. I noticed that his eyes were filled with weariness, yet also compassion. As I later learned, for several days and nights Jesus could not get adequate rest or sleep because of the crowds. They wanted to see him, touch him, and be touched by him.

Tom and I managed to be in the front of the crowd, so we were able to see where Jesus intended to go. The crowd moved slowly toward the shore of the beautiful Sea of Galilee, where we learned that Simon Peter, a follower of Jesus, had a large fishing boat that he also used for personal reasons. That explained why Jesus and his disciples left us to get into Simon Peter's boat and sail across the northern tip of the sea. Just a few miles away, they would land. I listened to Jesus until noon before he left.

Tom and I decided to eat lunch. That is, until a man close by shouted, "I know where they are going! If we hurry we can wade across the Jordan River where it flows into the Sea of Galilee, as it is shallow this time of the year. We can then go quickly to the place where Simon Peter's boat usually lands on the other side of the Sea of Galilee."

Some of the crowd suddenly started talking. "If we hurry, we can be there when the boat lands." Caught up in the emotion of the moment Tom and I started running to stay ahead of the crowd, although Tom was unhappy and complained about postponing lunch.

We came to the Jordan River where it empties into the Sea of Galilee and waded across the river at low tide. We ran as only teenagers can until we arrived just before Simon Peter's boat came to the shore. Tom and I helped some of the disciples out of the boat and one of them, named John, noticed me especially. Of course I still had the bag lunch.

Hungrier to hear and see Jesus than to eat, my lunch stayed in my bag. Suddenly it hit me. Can you imagine a teen being so engrossed in a religious service that they forget to eat? It happened to me and that's a miracle in itself.

The afternoon wore on as Jesus taught the people. Wonderful words fell from his lips. Jesus healed the sick. Those hurting in body and mind heard his words and felt his touch. His words and hands brought healing to tired minds and bodies. And all the while, he whispered words of comfort and earnest tones of concern as he expressed compassion for the needy. For me, Jesus fulfilled everything the prophets predicted about the messiah.

I stayed as close as I could with thousands of people thronging around Jesus. The apostle John let us stay close to Jesus because Tom and I had helped him get the boat to shore.

The evening was getting late. I needed to start toward home to make it before dark, yet something wouldn't let me leave. Tom felt the same,

The sun began to set in the west. The disciples told Jesus to send the people away so they could find food and lodging. Jesus then made a strange statement. Jesus told his disciples to give the people something to eat. They logically responded, "We don't have any food, or enough money, or even a place to buy food if we had the money." What happened next I never would have believed had I not seen and heard it for myself.

John the apostle looked at my lunch. Maybe he had a hunch about my lunch. Could it be a part of a miracle? John told Jesus that a teenage boy with five loaves of bread and two fish seemed to have the only food available.

Jesus looked at me tenderly. He knew how much a teenage boy loved to eat. Then Jesus said, "Ben"—he knew my name just like he knows yours—"would you give your lunch to me so I can feed the people?" How could I refuse?

"Here Jesus, take my lunch," I said.

The miracle happened. He took my lunch bag in his hands and looked toward heaven as he prayed a prayer of thanks for the food. Jesus opened my lunch bag and took out the five loaves of bread and two fish and starting breaking them into pieces. He put the disciple to work distributing the pieces to the crowd of people. Everyone ate until they could not eat another bite. And then the disciples picked up twelve baskets of broken pieces that were left over. They had enough for a meal the next day, and I had more in my lunch bag than when I had left home, since Jesus gave it back to me.

We returned home after dark. Mother, seeing my full bag, asked, "Why didn't you and Ben eat your lunch?"

"Mother you gave me a miracle today." I told her what Jesus did with my lunch. My life was changed that day, and Jesus owned it.

Jesus made one statement that stuck with me forever among many of the wonderful things he said and did that day. John the apostle remembered, and he alone in his gospel records this final statement Jesus made that day in John 6:12: "*When the people had eaten their fill, he said to his disciples, 'Gather the leftovers so nothing is wasted.'"*

Ben's Reactions

Ben reacted to a need by giving to Jesus what he had and believed that Jesus would in some way multiply what he gave. You and I can do that.

An Illustration from Personal Experience

We may possess very little by human standards like the young lad with five loaves and two fish, but if we obey the Lord, he provides adequately. Listen to part of my ministerial story, an experience that many ministers share when responding affirmatively to the Lord's call to serve him full-time in Christian service.

My call to ministry became a driving force in my decision to say "yes" to that call when I was twenty-seven years old. Married with two children ages seven and six, I initially resisted the call, partly because of some stories of how difficult it was to serve the Lord and provide for a family on a pastor's salary. The Scripture portion that contained a section of Jesus' words from the Sermon on the Mount persuaded me to trust my life's calling to the Lord. During a Sunday morning worship service, my pastor read the following Scripture intending to speak about stewardship. Yet it convicted my heart, soul, and mind to trust the Lord to provide for my family.

> *If God gives such attention to the appearance of wildflowers—most of which are never even seen—don't you think he'll attend to you, take pride in you, do his best for you? 31 What I'm trying to do here is to get you to relax, to not be so preoccupied with getting, so you can respond to God's giving. 32 People who don't know God and the way he works fuss over these things, but you know both God and how he works. 33 Steep your life in God-reality,*

God-initiative, God-provisions. Don't worry about missing out. You'll find all your everyday human concerns will be met.

34 Give your entire attention to what God is doing right now, and don't get worked up about what may or may not happen tomorrow. God will help you deal with whatever hard things come up when the time comes. (Matt 6:30–34)

The first thing in life is to give for the Lord's use as he deems best for you!

Mathematically these few examples I share do not exactly match our normal human scales of measurement.

1. I moved my family to a Christian college to prepare without a job. The Lord provided one.

2. Lacking the tuition money, a local business in my hometown paid my first two years of tuition.

3. Living on a pastor's salary when it came time for my children to attend college, I often had to borrow more money than my salary could provide to be paid back each semester. In unexplained ways, even to me today, the Lord provided speaking engagements, gifts, and other means of income to meet those expenses so that they could graduate debt-free. Of course, as students, they participated in work-study programs.

What do you possess today to present to the Lord Jesus Christ? Begin with giving Jesus all of you for his service. He will pray over you, bless you, and provide abundantly. It is still a day of possible miracles.

Though what Ben had at that time was small compared to the need to feed thousands of people, he gave it to Jesus.

Let Jesus pray for you and use you for his glory. Let nothing you only temporarily possess be wasted.

George the Goods Guy

18 One day one of the local officials asked him, "Good Teacher, what must I do to deserve eternal life?"

19 Jesus said, "Why are you calling me good? No one is good—only God. 20 You know the commandments, don't you? No illicit sex, no killing, no stealing, no lying, honor your father and mother."

21 He said, "I've kept them all for as long as I can remember."

22 When Jesus heard that, he said, "Then there's only one thing left to do: Sell everything you own and give it away to the poor. You will have riches in heaven. Then come, follow me."

23 This was the last thing the official expected to hear. He was very rich and became terribly sad. He was holding on tight to a lot of things and not about to let them go.

24 Seeing his reaction, Jesus said, "Do you have any idea how difficult it is for people who have it all to enter God's kingdom? 25 I'd say it's easier to thread a camel through a needle's eye than get a rich person into God's kingdom."

26 "Then who has any chance at all?" the others asked.

27 "No chance at all," Jesus said, "if you think you can pull it off by yourself. Every chance in the world if you trust God to do it."

LUKE 18:18–27

George the Goods Guy

WHETHER OR NOT YOU were born into a wealthy environment, a middle-class setting, or grew up poverty stricken, George's story, as he personally tells it, reminds us to consider our attitude toward our current possessions.

This is George's story as he might tell it today.

~

Born into a prosperous family, the oldest of six sons, I enjoyed the privileges that go with being the firstborn. Of the six sons, my personality was most like my father's.

Father worked hard. An honest and religious man, he faithfully took our family to the synagogue for worship. Yet his main ambition and interest was to seek first the goods of this world rather than God. I followed his example.

Business appealed to me. Father, shrewd but honest, raised and traded animals, acquired additional land for farming, and grew our possessions into a large estate.

Through the years, I watched and learned the ins and outs of the family businesses, enjoying every day of the various challenges. But then, at my young age of thirty, a crushing blow occurred in the family. Father died, leaving me, the eldest son, to fulfill the centuries-old tradition that the firstborn should take over and keep the family intact.

Fortunately, my love for my family and my business acumen allowed me to quickly settle the dividing of the estate after a thirty-day period of mourning. My part of the inheritance, two-sevenths, as the oldest son, meant receiving a larger portion than the other five sons, who received one seventh each.

Negotiating with my brothers to buy them out so we could keep the family farm and other business interests intact went very quickly. Part of the agreement meant furnishing them and their families with decent jobs with excellent wages in the future and a percentage of the future profits. We agreed and settled the estate. I loved my brothers and their families and sincerely looked after them materially. Unfortunately, following my father's example, I put business first and neglected my role as a spiritual leader

The farm continued to flourish. More and more animals, land, and rich harvests made our family quite wealthy. We enjoyed the good life. Our farm grew so large that to protect ourselves we had to fence it in from unwanted wild beasts and, yes, some people. Our philosophy seemed to be, "Plenty is good, but more is better!" But things were about to change when my treasured lifestyle would be exposed for what it was.

While I had been enjoying my reputation in the area as the "main man" and a rich guy, my mind kept recalling a boyhood friend named Lazarus. Strange!

As a young lad I played stickball and went swimming in the Jordan River with him. We even attended the same synagogue. Lazarus seemed more interested in God than in getting ahead in life, so we didn't have much in common as we grew older. I lost touch with Lazarus after our teen years and into manhood.

However, word came to me that sickness had dealt him a horrible blow as he began to suffer from a disease that would eventually take his life. Lazarus was poor, sick, and suffering. There was not much I could do about that. Besides I was rich, prosperous, and in good health. It was quite obvious where God's blessings were bestowed.

One day, returning from another successful business trip, my chariot passed through the gated entrance to our plush estate. Beside the gate a ragged, emaciated beggar sat asking for alms. He looked familiar. Could it be? It was! The beggar was my childhood friend Lazarus in this pitiful condition. My first impulse was to take him home with me, but I knew my wife would never allow someone as filthy and sick as Lazarus to enter our home. We had an outstanding and well-developed reputation to maintain in the community.

From that day on, my wife complained whenever she saw Lazarus outside our gate begging for alms. Little did she know that, occasionally, after we ate our big meal at noon, I instructed the servants to scrape the plates and bowls and quietly give the leftovers to Lazarus. It felt good to know I did a little something that really didn't cost me anything to help an old friend like Lazarus.

My family believed that if you succeeded in this life with material blessings, it indicated you were in good standing with God, now and for eternity. For us, earthly riches meant a combination of God's earthly and eternal blessings.

In a weekly business meeting of community leaders, these leaders began to talk about a young prophet named Jesus, who was about my age. They witnessed that he talked about eternal life with an authority never heard before. Some thought he might even be the messiah.

Certainly, Jesus would want to meet me, because as a successful business man in the area, I could help his ministry along by recommending him to my elite circle of young businessmen.

As a ruler in the business world, I enjoyed fellowship with another childhood friend, Nicodemus. He became a member of the religious Jewish ruling council. When our paths crossed, he also spoke about Jesus and his teachings. If Jesus could impress Nicodemus, he must be something special.

And while concentrating on this current world and accumulating more goods, in the back of my mind a serious thought kept coming into my focus—one day death would make its final call.

A friend came by to tell me that Lazarus had died. Life had dealt him a severe blow when he was struck down with life-draining sores. They said that, even up to the end of his life, Lazarus continued to love and trust God. That's hard to believe since God could have spared his suffering had he wanted to.

Lazarus's emotional state obviously had to be under intense stress. He might have said to himself, "If God really loved me, I would not be experiencing this horrible problem." Or Lazarus may have thought, "Maybe I don't love God enough and that is the reason for my suffering." However, like Job in the Old Testament, Lazarus kept his faith in God and was finally rewarded for his faith despite difficult circumstances that surrounded his earthly life, as I later found out.

Would I inherit eternal life? I faithfully went to the synagogue every Sabbath, unless business took me out of town. I memorized a lot of Moses' writings. And while I didn't regularly tithe, because

I needed the money to advance my personal kingdom, once in a while I would give some offerings. Surely doing all this would get me into heaven, wouldn't it? That answered my question. It made perfect sense to my father that riches proved God's approval, and my father proved to be right. The way to obtain eternal life must depend on me doing something.

Could Jesus answer my question? I was already doing everything humanly possible to live a productive life for myself and the family. I earned and inherited the family business, increasing it by leaps and bounds, through hard work and ingenuity. It was only logical that obtaining eternal life depended on me doing something.

When I met Jesus, a young man about my age, he shocked me by answering my question and told me what I must do to inherit eternal life.

Dressed in my finest business apparel of purple and fine linen, the crowd surrounding Jesus opened a path to let me come close to him. Jesus did not have any livestock, land, or a farm to sell, so the crowd was very curious, as I usually did not spend much time with others unless it possibly offered a potential profit to be made. They knew me and, more importantly, so did Jesus.

I called Jesus the Good Teacher and asked the important question: "What good thing must I do to inherit eternal life?" Jesus answered me indirectly at first and then provided the truth I needed to hear. He told me to obey the commandments. Eagerly I responded, "Which ones?" Jesus stated the last seven of the Ten Commandments concerning the Sabbath: care for parents; no murder; no adultery; no stealing; no false witnessing; and no covetousness. Confidently and proudly I replied, "I have kept all of these since I was a boy." And I had.

Jesus, while not stating the first three commandments about putting God first, having no idols or other gods, and keeping God's name holy, went straight to the heart of my problem. Jesus with his answer implied that being good does not mean making a life by only seeking material things. It means God first. Jesus told me to prepare for heaven by selling my goods and giving them to the poor. Deep down, I worshiped goods rather than God. I was George the Goods Guy.

No! A thousand times, no! This couldn't be true. I wouldn't accept it. After a lifetime of seeking the good life on earth, I couldn't give it up. I loved my current life. Maybe sometime in the future I would let God be first. Maybe!

Jesus looked at me that day with piercing eyes that shook my soul. I turned away very "sad." The Bible word "sad" that reveals my emotions describes mental anguish and distress. Jesus' requirement for eternal life shook me. God must be first in my life.

Not long afterward, a friend rushed into my office and said that I had to hear the story that Jesus was telling the crowds in town. I told him that I had heard all I needed to hear about Jesus, but he insisted that I listen, that it was a matter of life and death.

He said that Jesus told them the story of a rich man (Luke 12:16–21) whose ground produced a good crop. Great! There's that word "good" again. He said the man decided to tear down old barns, build newer ones, and feed his soul with food, drink, and entertainment. He sounded like a man after my own heart, until Jesus said that God called him a fool. And that he died that night. Jesus said that this is how it will be with anyone who stores up things for himself but is not rich toward God. I told my friend that I was not impressed, but he insisted that I let him relate the second story told about a rich man.

Jesus also told another story (Luke 16:19–31) about a rich man dressed in purple and fine linen living in luxury. And Lazarus also laid at his gate, begging.

The rich man died. Lazarus died. Lazarus received eternal life and the everlasting joys of heaven. The rich man landed in Hades, a place of torment.

Somehow, the rich man in Hades was able to see Lazarus in heaven standing next to Abraham. He begged for a personal benefit by having Lazarus bring him even one drop of water to ease his misery. The request was denied, as the reality of visiting either heaven or Hades was seen as closed to those in the opposite place.

Then the rich man asked for mercy for his five brothers. He had looked after them and their families for years. They did not need to come here. He implored Abraham to send Lazarus or someone from the dead to warn his brothers. Request denied. *"Abraham answered, 'They have Moses and the Prophets to tell them the score. Let them listen to them'"* (Luke 16:29).

And you, hearing my story today, have Moses and the prophets and in addition the Lord Jesus Christ. What is your excuse for not putting God first?

My friend asked what I thought about the other two stories about a rich man as told by Jesus. I told him I thought it was a cruel joke he was playing on me, like other jokes before, but this one tipped the scales. I told him to leave and never come back. My father believed that living a prosperous life and providing for the family would guarantee God's eternal blessings. My father was never wrong. Or was he? Jesus may have possibly referred only to me, or me and two other different men, in the three stories. Whether one man or three men, the three incidents as told by Jesus call for thoughtful reaction.

George's Reactions

1. George put goods first, possessed with the desire for more and more and more, ahead of God. Have you?

2. George enjoyed prestige and position more than God. Do you?

3. He was bothered about preparing for the hereafter, but he ignored the solution.

   George mainly prepared for the present only. For when a person dies a question often asked contains this general thought: "How much of this world's goods did they leave?" The obvious answer: "They left it all." Earth's goods cannot replace an eternal God.

When you have personal thoughts about life, after this one, what is or are your reaction(s)? I challenge you to react by putting God, through Jesus Christ, first in your life.

An Illustration from Personal Experience

Let me share with you a story about a "George the Goods Guy" type of man I knew about personally a number of years ago.

His family's two-story home was built around 1800. When I met this man, he was about seventy. This is how he lived in his pursuit of more.

In that small community as a young adult, he inherited a good portion of land, which he farmed with diligence. He married and had children, who helped him. But after reaching adulthood, they moved away.

He became obsessed with buying land. He sacrificed personally, never allowing himself or his family to spend more than needed, only for the bare necessities of life. They lived as very poor people despite the means to live better.

One story about him that stood out was that he would walk by the local grocery store in the small community and, seeing steak displayed in the window, would sincerely say, "I wish I could afford that." He could have bought the store if he had wanted to, but the love of even more land kept him bound from the slightest of life's pleasures. He lived by this rule, that he would only buy land and would never sell any land to anyone. Over a forty-to-fifty-year period of time, he accumulated approximately 75 percent of the land in that small community.

A small church needed a sliver of land about six feet wide and thirty feet long adjoining their property for some additional parking. They tried to buy it from him, as he owned an adjoining parcel of about sixty acres. He simply said, "I buy land; I don't sell it."

This person, with his love of land, prepared his will so that the land he owned would remain intact for one hundred years after his death and no development would or could take place in the community. He died. His family contested the will. Within three years after his death, houses began to appear as the family broke the will, and his dream died soon after he did.

If any one or more temporal desires directs your lifestyle instead of eternal values, remember that when you are gone, you are gone.

Laban the Leper Needs Love

One day in one of the villages there was a man covered with leprosy. When he saw Jesus he fell down before him in prayer and said, "If you want to, you can cleanse me."

13 Jesus put out his hand, touched him, and said, "I want to. Be clean." Then and there his skin was smooth, the leprosy gone.

14 Jesus instructed him, "Don't talk about this all over town. Just quietly present your healed self to the priest, along with the offering ordered by Moses. Your cleansed and obedient life, not your words, will bear witness to what I have done."

LUKE 5:12–16

LABAN (FICTIONAL NAME FOR the leper) tells his story about his healing by Jesus.

∼

Let me share with you the highs and lows that characterize my life. I enjoyed the best of life, and also experienced about the worse that life offers.

Born in Israel to a middle-class family in AD 1, we lived on a small farm inherited from my grandparents. The livestock that we raised and the variety of crops that we grew and harvested were more than enough to feed our family, which consisted of my parents, three brothers, and two sisters. I am the youngest.

My parents loved me and constantly showed their affection for me by holding and hugging me. Their touch brought feelings of safety and assurance to a little boy growing up with older brothers and sisters.

We didn't possess a lot of wealth by some standards, but we knew and enjoyed an abundance of love and felt safe and cared for. We simply loved each other, and more importantly, we loved Jehovah.

A small group of people lived on the outskirts of our town. My parents told me to stay away from them. They called these isolated people "lepers," an unclean people before God and society. I asked my father what being unclean meant. He responded that there were three general ways people of our religion were declared "unclean."

First—Someone was temporarily unclean (dirty) until a problem was removed by bathing and washing their clothes.

Second—A more serious sort of unclean occurred when contact was made with a human corpse. That defiled the person for seven days and was removed by bathing and washing the clothes,

Third—Uncleanness in the case of leprosy lasted for life, as no known cure existed for this type of uncleanness.

The concept of isolation from contact with society at large catches much of the meaning of uncleanness suffered by those afflicted with leprosy.

I questioned my father as to why or what happened to these people. He said, "Son, we are not sure of the cause or possible causes of their leprosy, but some of us think their disease means God is displeased with them personally. Whatever you do, if you happen to be close to one of them, do not touch them, for you could get leprosy from them."

What my father told me frightened me enough to stay away from lepers. However, from a distance, occasionally I would hear and see some of them walking and calling out, "Unclean, unclean." Hearing the words was scary enough, but when they got close enough to see, they presented a horrible physical sight. It gave me bad dreams at night, and I knew why.

When I was a little boy, I had a nervous twitch that always caused me to gently rub my ear lobes. So when a leper appeared without ear lobes, I just knew I had leprosy. Crying, I raced into my father's arms and told him I was a leper. After telling him about the nervous twitch that I had and the man without ears, he held me and said, "Son, you've had that twitch since you were two years old. If that was the first sign of the disease in you, there would be other body parts missing by now."

I said, "You mean like some of the others out there?"

"Yes, but for now, son, you are young, healthy, and much loved."

Years later when encountering a leper, I still cringed to see missing or partial arms, legs, and fingers. But the worst of all these horrible sights was the way leprosy disfigured faces. Whenever I could, I always turned my eyes away when approaching these stricken, sad souls.

I remembered that the law of Moses gave instructions about leprosy. The law described how to diagnose it and how to deal with the leper. But the law said nothing about how to treat it medically, or cure it, not even how to cleanse it.

Lepers simply became a remote background of my life. I cared for lepers and even prayed for them, and wanted to help them. But following father's admonition, I stayed away from any contact with them.

Eventually, Sarah, the girl of my dreams, came into my life. After providing a proper dowry to her father, we married and started our own family. Her father's family, like mine, showed great love for each other. They greeted each other warmly with hugs and encouraging words. Two loving families wanted their children when they married to experience the love, respect, and care that they enjoyed. I didn't have to worry, as Sarah's family had the same values as mine. Two caring families who loved each other, but loved Jehovah above all else, gave their blessing for Sarah and me to begin our own family, knowing we would follow their example.

During our first ten years of marriage, Jehovah blessed us with two boys and a girl. The boys became mother's boys and the little girl became a father's girl. In mine and Sarah's immediate family, love abounded from our shared expressions of love, as it had in our parents' homes. At this point in time, it seemed Jehovah smiled with extra blessing on my family. The family business flourished with no hint of anything going wrong. But one night, I awakened in pain.

It felt like just a little more than a minor ache. I decided to work it off the next day. Unfortunately, it continued to get worse. So rather than tell my family, after several weeks, I went to a friend who was quite gifted in medical things. After telling him where it hurt, he examined me by asking how long I'd had this pain. I told him just a short while and that the pain seemed minimal at first. My friend exclaimed, "I think you need to go to the priest. You may have the beginning of leprosy."

That just couldn't be! Me! Impossible! God loved me! I loved him! He had prospered my father and mother and my wife's family. Impossible!

I immediately went to the priest, who confirmed by the directions given in the law of Moses that every sign indicated leprosy. He instructed me to go directly to the lepers' camp and stay there. It was actually a death sentence.

I pleaded with the priest to let me go and personally tell my wife and children. He said I could, but as I approached them I had to quickly shout out, "Unclean, unclean" making sure I did not touch them in anyway.

As I headed home, I met lifelong and dear friends who started to come up and greet me as before with a hug or a handshake, but I had to shout out, "Unclean, unclean." They backed off and gave me a wide path.

Arriving outside my home, I again cried out, "Unclean, unclean." My wife ran hurriedly out of the house to greet me. I told her, "I'm a leper. Do not come near me because you have to take care of the children from this day forward." She cried. My children also ran toward me, but I had to tell them to stay away from their father. Seeing their mother cry, they started crying even though they did not fully understand what had happened that would change their life forever. That was my final goodbye at my home to my family. From that moment on, my family and society realistically considered me a dead man, though still alive.

Can you even imagine the mental anguish I experienced that day and every day and night thereafter? Never again could I hold my wife in my arms. Never again could I hold my children in my arms or let them sit on my lap. Never—never—again.

After I left that day, I would forever see my wife standing in the yard holding the hands of the children. The children didn't understand, but Sarah did. A living but dead husband she could never love with even the slightest affectionate touch or kiss.

I wondered if Jehovah had ever loved me. The day before, I'd believed that he did, and even in the days before that one I had felt and seen the light of his love. Those days contained the light of love. But my physical and emotional suffering soon dimmed and almost snuffed out the fact or possibility of love.

Leprosy began to consume me slowly, piece by piece. My physical and emotional torture became a perpetual nightmare. The loss of family tormented my mind day and night. Sarah would often bring the children to the edge of the lepers' camp so I could see them from afar. I called out to them, but I couldn't show them my love as before. Over and over I would call out, "Daddy loves you. Do you still love me?" Sarah and the children kept shouting that they did.

As time passed, in some ways, I dreaded for them to come and see me. My hands became disfigured as fingers began to rot and fall off. My facial appearance became so hideous that I dreaded to even look at my reflection in a basin of water. I could still walk, stumbling along with several missing toes.

But in my mind, and understandably so, I felt forsaken and utterly separated from Jehovah. My religious training taught me by strong implication that this ghastly disease had come upon me as a mark of divine displeasure. My suffering made me wonder if God's love even existed for someone like me.

One day in the midst of my agony, stories began to circulate about a young rabbi doing miraculous works never seen before.

Some declared that he healed the sick, made the lame to walk, opened the eyes of the blind, and even raised dead people. And I, to all intents, qualified as a dead man. At first these stories meant nothing to me, for everyone already considered me dead, and I joined them in their thinking.

A few days later, a traveler came close to me, and though I cried out the traditional warning, "Unclean, unclean," the traveler with an excited voice cried out, "Yesterday, I was blind! Today I can see! I met Jesus of Nazareth and he cured me. He can cure your leprosy!" A hope long dormant awakened when I heard the man's words. *This physician can cure me. Maybe if he just touched me, I would be clean.*

Blemished and an outcast, I longed to see the love and compassion in the eyes of my wife, my children, other family members, and friends. I wanted to be held and hugged and experience human touch again. I wanted to be healed. Could Jesus heal me? It seems from their testimony that Jesus possessed miraculous power. But would he love me enough to use that power to heal me? I, Laban a leper, had to make an effort. What could I lose? It was not enough to sit idly by and wish. Technically already dead, why not take a chance?

When Jesus came by, I went toward him. Yet I approached beset by many doubts. *Will Jesus even receive me? The crowd may not let me get close. His disciples might not welcome a leper in the midst of a mighty national movement.* Fear filled my total being.

Yet I came, stumbling as best I could, toward Jesus, shouting "Unclean, unclean." Falling at his feet, I said, "If you want to, you can cleanse me." It was not too difficult for me to believe in the mighty power of God when I observed the created world and its creatures. Yet life's misfortunes caused me to doubt the love of Jesus Christ. Again, I said, "If you want to, you can cleanse me."

I came with an open honesty, and Jesus had compassion for me. He didn't repel me. I could hardly stay composed when I realized what Jesus did even before he healed me. He touched me while still a leper. Jesus loved me.

Jesus reached out his hand and touched me. "I want to. Be clean!" Immediately my leprosy left me. He did love me.

Jesus touched me with a spontaneous act of love. When he healed me, Laban the leper, an awareness filled my soul that love still existed.

That day after seeing the priest and being declared clean according to the law of Moses, I rushed home. Instead of calling out "Unclean, unclean" as I approached the house, I called out with a clear, loud voice, "Honey, I'm home. I'm healed. I'm home for good. Jesus healed me. Come quickly and bring the children. I need a hug. Look at my face—normal. Look at my hands and feet—normal. My leprosy is gone forever."

Laban's Reactions

Laban's personal thoughts about his condition may have been something like this: *Why did this happen to me? What can I do? Can I take care of my family?* My observations about Laban's reactions are as follows:

Laban accepted his condition as best he could. That is a start.

He kept his faith, though very dim due to his condition.

At his first opportunity, he sought help from Jesus.

And like Laban, when life seems to come to a dead-end road, our only hope remains Jesus, the Son of God. And in those times, we need a big God. He is available.

An Illustration from Personal Experience

Let me share with you about my friend George who overcame difficult obstacles because he believed God would heal and use him.

In his early adult life (ages sixteen to thirty-four) George lived a rough life. In his early thirties, he met his future wife, and she persuaded him to go to church with her. Eventually he accepted Christ and became a devout Christian. Then he approached the pastor and related that he felt God's call to preach. In that system of church government, a pastor had to recommend George to the local church board, and they in turn would recommend the candidate to the state governing board for a beginning license. But there was a big problem with George. Besides being a tall and heavy person, his speaking voice was very shrill. No way could George be a minister. But he was firmly adamant about the Lord's call.

He enrolled in the denominational college to prepare for the ministry despite a limited education and his high, shrill voice. The leaders of the college and the professors all questioned George's qualifications to be a minister or successfully pastor a church.

One Sunday night when entering the college church, George's hip broke, but not from a fall. Doctors discovered that George had a condition where the body would keep growing until he died from the growing. His hip bones could not support his growth. They transferred him to a major medical center as a person to study, as only about seven known cases like George's existed in the world at that time in the 1960s. They treated him without charge to stop the total growth of his body and continued that for the rest of his life. As of this writing, George is now ninety years old.

Something else happened besides regulating his growth. George's voice level became very normal. Gone was the shrill voice, as it was replaced with a well-toned male voice.

George started out to be a minister with very little to offer, as people would judge him. But over a forty-year period of ministry serving six small congregations, the attendance doubled, and the churches became financially stable. George had an ability to lead building programs where needed. Three new churches, a pioneer church project with a church and parsonage, and two new parsonages were erected because of his God-anointed leadership

A man with physical limitations, but surrendered to God's call, bypassed human opinions and succeeded.

And today, you personally may feel singled out as not worth very much because of real or perceived limitations. If the Lord calls and touches your life, miracles can happen. One result when the Lord honors you will be that he has to get the glory, because there is no way you could accomplish what the Lord ordains for your life without his powerful touch.

Charlie's Carriage and Cart Shop

When Jesus left the field, he entered their meeting place. 10 There was a man there with a crippled hand. They said to Jesus, "Is it legal to heal on the Sabbath?" They were baiting him.

11 He replied, "Is there a person here who, finding one of your lambs fallen into a ravine, wouldn't, even though it was a Sabbath, pull it out? 12 Surely kindness to people is as legal as kindness to animals!" 13 Then he said to the man, "Hold out your hand." He held it out and it was healed. 14 The Pharisees walked out furious, sputtering about how they were going to ruin Jesus.

15 Jesus, knowing they were out to get him, moved on. A lot of people followed him, and he healed them all.

MATTHEW 12:9–15

MY NAME IS CHARLIE, and I lived during the lifetime of Jesus Christ. But that is getting ahead of my story.

I came from a family who seemed obsessed with the name Charlie; hence, I represent the fourth generation of Charlies, and my oldest son will carry on the legacy.

As I pondered my heritage, I realized that something had to be extremely significant to want the name to be passed on to future generations. But what?

I found the answer through my carriage and cart repair business, inherited from my father after he died. Not only had he taught me how to build and repair carts and carriages, he taught me how to run my shop with excellence while offering fair prices for the work done. No need to advertise like most folks today. Word of mouth was enough to spread my reputation well beyond my village. I wonder if that could be said of most of your businesses today.

Don't think for a minute there were no problems. Quite the contrary, especially when reliable carts were needed to transport animal sacrifices to the temple. You would think the temple would be the one place where honesty and fairness were essential. Not so in our culture!

I think the best way to say this is that greed not only took over the sanctity of the sacrifice but the sacredness of the temple itself. The priests did as God commanded—they demanded the sacrifices to be the best animals available. Unbeknownst to many, they didn't sacrifice all of them. Instead, they built up a small flock to be used to gain money from unsuspecting folks who came from afar to honor the Lord. When a traveler presented the appropriate sacrifice, the priests would simply say it was not good enough. Being the "kindhearted" priests that they were, they offered to sell the traveler one of their acceptable offerings. You guessed it! The acceptable animal would be sold at an extremely exorbitant price. The travelers and often the local people had no choice. Now they had to make two sacrifices: a personal financial loss and that of an animal they had brought.

I am ashamed that I had to reveal that to you, but then I wonder if greed has also crept into some of your places of worship. More and more I am beginning to see that through the years man's baser instincts have not changed much. It certainly provokes much heart- and soul-searching.

My struggle was how to be the man God wanted me to be amid all the corruption surrounding my family and business. I knew I was not responsible for the actions of others. God had taught me through the teachings of Moses and the prophets that my responsibility was to him—that we should have no other gods before him. That is why I insisted that my family faithfully observe the Sabbath and study the sacred Scriptures. I also taught them to make and keep family traditions, what I call the bonding phase of family living.

For our family, it was always a time of various contests, especially those where the men could show off their strengths. I confess that I liked these the most because I became somewhat of a legend, known especially for my arm and leg strength. Of course, there was also music, laughter, plenty of food, and simply enjoying being together. Life was good! That is, until I awoke one morning feeling extremely weak.

I tried to shake it off, as a man should, but when I started to lift a hammer, things became dim, and I had double vision. I didn't know what was happening. My mind became confused. When I slowly sank down to the ground, my sons ran over to help. I tried to speak but couldn't. My right leg and arm lost strength. I could hear my sons asking what was wrong, but my words were slurred. It seemed as if my mind and my tongue operated like two separate parts of my body with no coordination. I now know that I'd had a stroke.

Time passed as days became weeks, then months, and then time melted into years. I slowly recovered. My right leg could support me, though I was left with a slight limp. My mental capacity was stable to the point that I could once again run the business with my sons. I diligently exercised my right hand and arm, but the lack of blood and muscle activity left me dependent on others daily.

Through all of this, I faithfully trusted Jehovah and attended the synagogue. The rituals often bored me, but I still went, hoping against hope that something could be done for me. I knew that even when life handed out unwanted problems, not just the physical ones, the Lord was faithful and knew what was best for my life.

On one particular Sabbath, a man named Jesus was there and started preaching and teaching God's word. I had never before heard truths expounded so clearly, so clearly that even I could understand them. Just the look on his face was enough to hold my attention. I wondered if others were as rapt with his teaching as I was.

In noticing others who had come, I spotted the Herodians and other religious leaders congregated together with nothing but disdain in their words. Their faces expressed a deep-rooted anger in their hearts. I found out later that they had one goal—to catch Jesus in some activity or statement they could use against him. Why? Because he was exposing the corruption of self-serving religious leaders, not just in the temple but in the religious system itself. All this at the expense of the helpless masses.

As I continued listening to Jesus, I remembered hearing that he had healed others with just a word or a touch. Could that happen to me? As if in an answer to an unspoken prayer, Jesus came over to my side. The religious officials watched him intently. If Jesus healed me, according to those leaders, he would be working on the Sabbath, breaking a very serious rule.

Jesus asked me to stand, and when I did, a renewed energy swept through my right leg. A miracle! Jesus asked me to walk and stand in the middle of the synagogue so that everyone could see that I no longer had a limp. He knew it would create dissention among those religious leaders, and he was right. They thought they could trap him by asking him if it was lawful to heal on the Sabbath.

> He replied, "Is there a person here who, finding one of your lambs fallen into a ravine, wouldn't, even though it was a Sabbath, pull it out? 12 Surely kindness to people is as legal as kindness to animals!" (Matt 12:11–12)

They remained silent because the answers to the questions were obvious.

Then Jesus spoke again, and he said words that have remained etched in my mind for the past two thousand years. He said, "*Hold out your hand.*" I wanted to, and I needed to, but in each of the years following my stroke, all efforts failed. Jesus' look—his outstretched hand—all dared me to try once more. When I lifted my arm and took his hand, both were made whole once again. Another miracle! How blessed! Just for the record, even had Jesus not healed me physically, I would still worship him because he healed the most important part of me—my soul!

Life is good once again. It would be so easy to bask in the glow of restored health. Easy to think that faithfully attending the synagogue and memorizing the Sacred Scriptures guaranteed that problems in every area of our lives would turn out favorably. You and I both know that isn't true and never will be true as long as imperfect humans occupy the world. So what then should we do?

Charlie's Reactions

Even when dealt a devastating blow, he still remained faithful and worshiped his Lord.

Charlie believed in Jesus Christ for healing of body and soul. That is promised in Isa 53:5:

> But it was our sins that did that to him,
> that ripped and tore and crushed him—our sins!
> He took the punishment, and that made us whole.
> Through his bruises we get healed.

And the same promise is repeated in 1 Pet 2:23–24:

> They called him every name in the book and he said nothing back. He suffered in silence, content to let God set things right. 24 He used his servant body to carry our sins to the Cross so we could be rid of sin, free to live the right way. His wounds became your healing.

An Illustration from Personal Experience

Charlie the carriage and cart maker was a wealthy fictional character, but I want to share with you a Charlie I knew, and how he reacted to a challenging turn of events in his family life that he shared with his wife, Norma.

Charlie Funderburk was born in South Carolina. But after serving in the US Navy during World War II, he settled in Gastonia, North Carolina, with his wife, Norma.

Charlie started a tire store and playfully named it the "Nobody Tire Store," owned by Mister Nobody. His tire store became one of the most successful in the area. People appreciated his self-depreciating humor with the unique store name, but most of all they valued his Christian character reflected in his honest business dealings. However, Charlie excelled even more with his positive reaction to a major challenge in his family life. Charlie and Norma had been married for fifteen years and had welcomed two daughters during that time. But then they were blessed with a son. Chip was born with developmental and intellectual disabilities. Outwardly, Chip was a handsome young man who appeared normal, but in reality he faced a lifetime of problems due to his disabilities. His parents were almost forty and wondered how Chip would be best cared for if they preceded him in death. They had personal resources to provide for him in the future, but their dream went beyond their own family.

Charlie, encouraged by Norma and a desire to meet the needs of others in similar life situations, began a process in the 1970s of working with local and state officials to meet those needs. The basic plan was to build and staff residential homes where four to six of those with intellectual disabilities could live with a house parent. After several years of hard work, what was once just a dream became a reality, as he now knew that Chip, if still alive, would be taken care of if he and Norma passed away before Chip.

Both Charlie and Norma have now died. But they left behind as a result of their labors, along with others', Gaston Residential Services, Inc., which supports and empowers people with developmental and other disabilities to live their lives as respected members of their community. Today, there are twenty residential care homes serving the Gastonia, North Carolina, area. Other communities have used their model as a guide.

Charlie Funderburk took a disappointment and turned it into a vehicle whereby many other people are being blessed today by his leadership. He served terms as the president of both the Gaston County and North Carolina State Associations for Retarded Citizens.

Often into every life there comes an unexpected tragedy. Let us consider reacting positively like Charlie and Norma did. Today, Chip and many others enjoy a positive and meaningful life despite their personal limitations due to Charlie and Norma's effort not just for their son but for others as well.

Judas—Confessor of Jehovah

When it was time, he sat down, all the apostles with him, 15 and said,
"You've no idea how much I have looked forward to eating this Passover
meal with you before I enter my time of suffering. 16 It's the last one I'll
eat until we all eat it together in the kingdom of God."

17 Taking the cup, he blessed it, then said, "Take this and pass it
among you. 18 As for me, I'll not drink wine again until the kingdom of
God arrives."

19 Taking bread, he blessed it, broke it, and gave it to them, saying,
"This is my body, given for you. Eat it in my memory."

20 He did the same with the cup after supper, saying, "This cup is the
new covenant written in my blood, blood poured out for you.

21 "Do you realize that the hand of the one who is betraying me is at
this moment on this table? 22 It's true that the Son of Man is going down
a path already marked out—no surprises there. But for the one who turns
him in, turns traitor to the Son of Man, this is doomsday."

23 They immediately became suspicious of each other and began
quizzing one another, wondering who might be about to do this.

LUKE 22:14–23

FOR THE FIRST TIME in my life, I, Judas, feel the need for complete honesty. Isn't that just like us weak mortals when we know

that death is inevitable? I am Judas, the worst of all sinners, the arrogant apostle who sat beside Jesus at the Lord's Supper and then sentenced him to death by betraying him to the religious authorities. Actually, it is not his death that is prompting me to write this—it's mine! I'm asking my son, Joel, to read the following account of my life, hoping for but not expecting a favorable response. Call it "coming clean."

~

It's quite ironic that I should be named Judas, especially since it means "Confessor of Jehovah" or "Praise Jehovah." Of course, my parents had no inkling of how I would betray this heritage.

You see, Judas is a Greek name, the same as the Hebrew name of Judah, our tribal founder. Tracing the line further, we descended from the same tribe as Jesus, and I was the only disciple from the tribe of Judah. This gives you a hint as to where my life of entitlement is going.

Actually, if anyone had a reason to be proud, it was my father, Simon Iscariot, a faithful, well-respected worshiper of God, or as you would call him today, a faithful Jew. I have to mention this because it was my father's wish for me to be like him, following Jehovah's ways, possibly becoming a prophet or preacher. That's why he named me what he did, "Confessor of Jehovah." Sadly, I did nothing but bring shame and disgrace to my name.

As a young boy growing up in Judea, a few miles south of Jerusalem, I worked with my father in his business. Father knew instinctively how to trade goods, animals, and land for profit. He was an honest man, setting a good example by making a fair deal for both sides. Those who did business with him not only respected his good character, but also his loyalty to Jehovah. He never missed setting aside the tithe on his profits—all faithfully given to the temple and the priests.

In looking back on my life, maybe I could in part blame my parents for my future failures, which you obviously already know about. I was a favored child who was indulged more than I should have been. My parents loved me, yet failed to exercise firm discipline when needed. I don't want to brag, but Jehovah gifted me a genial personality and leadership abilities, which brought me to the forefront of many activities. Unfortunately, I took personal credit for these attributes, forgetting the source of those gifts.

I remember in those early years how traveling prophets would come through our village with messages from Jehovah. I did listen to them and even once in a while followed one of them until the attraction faded. They soon disappeared from public view as well as from mine. Still remembering the significance of my name and believing it was almost a sign, I looked for a religious position that would take me to the top of the prophetic profession. Of course, it would have to be in the style I wanted for me and my family.

Speaking of my family, I married Rebekah in my late twenties. Within the next six years, we were blessed with two girls, Sarah and Rachel, and one son, Joel, who is already known to you. I loved my wife and children and wanted only the very best for them and myself. Isn't that the way a husband should feel—nothing but the best to keep up the "image"? I was still working with my father when I heard about a new prophet named Jesus from Nazareth of Galilee. Word quickly spread about his teachings, his healings, his words of authority, and his words of wisdom. Such teachings had never before been uttered by any other prophet. I wondered if this was the messiah that I had been hearing about while attending services in the synagogue. If so, he would be the exact prophet that I needed to get close to so that my spiritual, physical, and material needs could be met.

I won't bore you with the tactics I used to get Jesus' attention; however, I did go to hear him and made sure that he noticed me. It wasn't hard because he identified me immediately by my southern accent as being one of his own tribe of Judah. Jesus chose me as one of his twelve disciples. I made sure he recognized my abilities in a modest way, unlike Simon Peter, who spoke loudly and with authority, yet many times without reason. I made sure that when I spoke, it was tempered and only when needed.

Finally, the time came to be sent out among the people. Time to live up to my name. I might not be a prophet, but I was definitely a preacher. We went out two by two on preaching and healing missions. When I preached, people responded. When I prayed for the sick, they experienced healing. God's power flowed through me as his instrument. I certainly was fulfilling my name as "Confessor of Jehovah." Why, then, did I have a gnawing sensation redirecting my thoughts away from my ministry?

Though I served as treasurer of the apostles, I worried about the financial future of my family. I questioned where the money was coming from that was put in the apostles' treasury. How did Jesus take offerings where he preached? Did the other disciples pass their hats to the crowds or go through the crowds collecting an offering? Did Jesus tell the crowds to give him their tithes instead of giving them to the temple? Obviously he wouldn't do that. I remember a time when he said to the religious leaders,

> *You're hopeless, you religion scholars and Pharisees!*
> *Frauds! You keep meticulous account books, tithing on every nickel and dime you get, but on the meat of God's Law,*
> *things like fairness and compassion and commitment—the*
> *absolute basics!—you carelessly take it or leave it. Careful*
> *bookkeeping is commendable, but the basics are required.*
> (Matt 23:23)

Jesus was quite strict in telling me that a tithe of all the moneys collected by the apostles should go to the temple—that was fulfilling the law. The rest was kept in a treasury bag to help the poor. Once again, that disturbing feeling crept into my mind. I worked hard. My family was not suffering, but they certainly weren't living the life that was due them considering my status as one of the chosen twelve to be with Jesus. Plus, I was chosen to be the treasurer for the apostles. Only I knew how much money was in the treasury bag; it was so easy to keep some for myself, especially since other signs of entitlement were there. Jesus chose me—yes, me! I didn't ask for his favor like the mother of James and John, who wanted her sons to have seats of honor in heaven with Jesus. That really set me off!

I knew the law. I knew all the Scriptures calling for sinners to repent. I knew that stealing was wrong, and I knew Jesus knew what

I was doing, yet he continued to give me time to come clean. But I kept remembering how hard I worked—so much harder than the others. The voices in my head continued to plague me: "The significance of your name has been fulfilled thus far. Think how the money would improve your status and the well-being of your family." Over and over the words played in my mind. "You deserve this!"

At the last Passover meal, Jesus said one of us would betray him. He knew I was guilty, but instead of naming me as his betrayer, he said he would reveal it by a sign. He said, "It is the one to whom I will give this piece of bread when I have dipped it into the dish." He gave it to me, Judas Iscariot, the one who betrayed the innocent Jesus.

After betraying Jesus later that night, guilt flooded my soul. I tried to return the money they paid me for his betrayal, but it was refused. My mind was reeling with ill-timed thoughts. Everyone would know what I truly was—a thief, traitor, liar, self-seeking sinner who set himself above all others, even ignoring what Jesus told us earlier. Jesus said a man should deny himself—to forget self and his own interests. Jesus was even more compelling when he said to save a temporal life was to lose it, but to lose the temporal life was to find everlasting life. I willingly chose the temporal life. Too late!

I never once considered the disgrace of my sins that would follow my parents for the rest of their innocent lives. Hear me now, those of you who are listening. No one is to blame for another's actions. To say otherwise is to forget the words of Jesus from the Sermon on the Mount, recorded in Matt 7:1–2.

> Don't pick on people, jump on their failures, criticize their faults—unless, of course, you want the same treatment.
> 2 That critical spirit has a way of boomeranging.

My family deserves no shunning or other ill-deserved treatment. They had absolutely no knowledge of my thoughts and actions. I am the only one who deserves punishment for my sins.

Judas's Reactions

He tried to return the money and find forgiveness by attempting to undo the wrong committed. Judas discovered yielding to greed brought with it guilt, shame, and loss of life, both to the innocent and the guilty!

Sometimes when we think our conscience is reasoning sinful action, it may be from the one who comes to steal, kill, and destroy us—Satan. Judas discovered that too late!

An Illustration from Personal Experience

A woman, now in her sixties and a member of the church I served as pastor, once came to me and shared her heartbreaking story about her son.

As a child, he would steal things from other children and his parents. Appropriate discipline only temporarily stopped his bad behavior. His nature was to be deceitful and take advantage of others. Many times during his childhood and teen years, his parents bailed him out of serious trouble with people and the authorities. Nothing they tried stopped or changed his propensity to steal and take unlawful advantage of others, including his parents.

His father died. As an adult, this son was arrested several times and spent several years in prison. He then finally moved to another state and occasionally would call his mother, usually to ask for money. Sometimes she sent him some out of her limited retirement income.

Then one day the phone rang. It was her son. He said, "Mom, I'm in jail charged with murder. A friend of mine recently got a check for $1,800 dollars, which he cashed, and they are accusing me of killing him for the money. Mom, I didn't do it. Can you help me?"

After relating this brief story of her son's life, this mother made an extremely sad statement. "Pastor, I know he said he didn't murder anyone, but I know he did. What shall I do?"

She did her best to help him, but he was found guilty and sentenced to thirty years in prison for murder.

If you, as you read these stories, have a nature that acts as Judas's did, your only hope is to turn your life over to Jesus Christ and be born again with a new nature. Repent. Restart. Live free of your sinful nature.

Tim the Transformed Thief

LET ME INTRODUCE MYSELF. After living in heaven for nearly two thousand years, the Lord Jesus allowed me the privilege of coming back to earth to share my testimony with you today. My name is Tim, though you usually refer to me another way in the Bible.

I was born in Bethlehem one year before Jesus Christ came to earth. Being born a year before Jesus Christ allowed me to escape King Herod's paranoia that a newborn baby boy would replace him as king. He ordered all the male babies two years old and younger to be put to death. My father and mother often thanked Jehovah, as they prayed, for their son escaping Herod's insane insecurity.

My parents faithfully took me to the synagogue. Their forward faith included believing the messiah would come one day soon and deliver our nation from Roman occupation and oppression. When Roman soldiers would mistreat and malign my parents as worthless, my intense hatred for them became an obsession. *Messiah, please come.* But until then, I would take action.

I grew up with two neighborhood friends, Bob and Jim, and together we became a trio of teenage pranksters. Roman soldiers were our targets, and we stole from them when there was an opportunity. Bob became our leader, and we followed his directions.

As we grew into manhood, so did the level of our crimes, despite the tearful warnings of my parents. Bob brought us together with others of like mind and created a gang of thieves. We robbed and murdered Roman soldiers as an act of rebellion, and eventually we did the same to anyone else who got in our way. As a gang, united, we felt invincible. Rome should beware of us, for we would bring about its downfall in our country.

Then we began to hear about a prophet named Jesus Christ, who miraculously healed the sick, spoke wondrous words of encouragement, and challenged people to live worthy lives in ways never heard before. People began to ponder, and with good reasons, whether this could be the promised messiah. Could it be possible that my parent's faith in Jehovah's promise of a messiah would be fulfilled in this Jesus? Sometimes our gang followed the crowds from afar as they gathered around Jesus to see miracles and hear him speak.

One day we heard him give what you call today the "Sermon on the Mount." It touched my heart. But the peer pressure of the gang with Bob as our leader kept me from changing my dangerous and defiant lifestyle.

Our gang continued to move about Israel, plundering and sometimes killing. The Roman authorities wanted to catch us and put us to death. They planned a well-designed trap to catch the entire gang. But, on that fateful Wednesday night, they only captured the three of us, Bob, Jim, and me.

Roman justice moves swiftly. Arrested on a Wednesday night, we were brought to trial on Thursday morning, just before Passover the next day. The trial lasted less than an hour. The three of us received a sentence of death by crucifixion. Bob, our leader, you know as Barabbas. We would be crucified the next day. No court of appeals existed to offer any hope. We would die the on Calvary without any hope of mercy to delay our execution.

The soldiers severely scourged us with whips until our backs became blobs of bloody flesh. Then they took us to our cells for the night.

The Holy Bible records our crucifixion with these words:

> Two other men, both criminals, were also led out with him
> (Jesus Christ) to be executed. When they came to the place
> called the Skull, there they crucified him along with the
> criminals—one on his right, the other on his left.

Jesus said, "Father, forgive them, for they do not know what they are doing."

And they divided up his clothes by casting lots. The people stood watching, and the rulers even sneered at him. They said, "He saved others; let him save himself if he is the Christ of God, the Chosen One." The soldiers also came up and mocked him. They offered him wine vinegar and said, "If you are the king of the Jews, save yourself." There was a written notice above him, which read: THIS IS THE KING OF THE JEWS.

One of the criminals who hung there hurled insults at him: "Aren't you the Christ? Save yourself and us!"

But the other criminal rebuked him. "Don't you fear God," he said, "since you are under the same sentence? We are punished justly, for we are getting what our deeds deserve. But this man has done nothing wrong."

Then he said, "Jesus, remember me when you enter your kingdom."

Jesus answered him, "I tell you the truth, today you will be with me in paradise." (Luke 23:32–43)

In that dark, damp, and dismal prison, we knew the time for our crucifixion drew near with every passing second. The slow and yet swift night of pain and dread passed without sleep. Our execution day appointed by the judge dawned, and death awaited the three of us with no hope for escape.

Early that fateful Friday morning, we heard a loud voice boom, "BRING OUT THE PRISONERS."

In the past, our gang would pass by the hill called Calvary, the place of the skull, so named because the hill was shaped like a skull. Now our bones would soon be a part of Calvary's carnage.

Bob, known to you as Barabbas, became the most notorious of our gang. That prompted what happened. During the night, Bob could hear people shouting loudly, "RELEASE BARABBAS TO US BUT CRUCIFY JESUS CHRIST." With those shouts, hope rose in my gang leader's wicked heart. He knew the religious custom that during the observance of Passover a prisoner facing death could be released.

You remember the rest of the story. If not, let me tell you. Barabbas goes free and fervently flees as fast as he can away from Jerusalem, lest the authorities decide to keep him in custody for his crimes.

The Roman soldiers remove Jim and me from our cells and give us our personal crosses, instruments of death for us to carry to Calvary.

A third prisoner soon joins us whom at first I did not recognize.

It is Jesus Christ. He picks up and carries the cross that was Barabbas's and would die that day on a cross meant for Barabbas. Jesus walks wearily, carrying his cross. He's endured a mock trial, beatings, and a sleepless night. Matthew's gospel states it vividly in chapter 27 and verse 30: *"Then they spit on him and hit him on the head with the stick."*

The weight of the cross Jesus carries bends his bruised and bleeding back. But I believe that the weight of Jesus' cross in no way matched the weight of the world's sins he carried.

In front of us, a herald carried a placard publicly proclaiming our crimes. For Jim and I, the placard read "robber" and "murderer."

The herald's sign in front of Jesus Christ carried an inscription written in three languages, Latin, Greek, and Hebrew, so everyone attending the Passover feast would be able to read it. It read, "THIS IS THE KING OF THE JEWS."

The chief priest, a Sadducee, objected and wanted written in addition, "THIS MAN PROCLAIMED HE WAS THE KING OF THE JEWS." But Pilate the governor refused and the writing remained "THIS IS THE KING OF THE JEWS."

Our staggering death procession walks toward Calvary. The streets of Jerusalem were filled that day with religious pilgrims attending the ancient feast of Passover, as they celebrated deliverance fourteen hundred years before from Egyptian bondage. Some of them quietly prayed, "Do it again, Jehovah, and deliver us from Roman occupation."

The procession attracts the curious who want to see a crucifixion. Priests who initiated the false charges that led to Jesus' death sentence cry out like a rabble mob, forgetting their usual outward display of pious dignity as they shout insults and ridicule. Their hatred was undeniable.

Near the gate of the city, Jesus Christ, weakened by his ordeal, falls beneath the weight of the cross, and Simon of Cyrene carries the cross for Jesus the rest of the way.

We reach Calvary, the place of crucifixion. Clothing is removed from our bodies. Our crosses fall to the ground. Strong Roman soldiers hold us down on our personal crosses. Nails quickly pierce our hands and feet while we fill the early morning air with screams of anguish. But Jesus keeps repeating a prayer *"Father, forgive them; they don't know what they're doing"* (Luke 23:34).

A peg on each cross served as a seat to lend support to our bodies lest the weight of the body tear it from the cross. Finally the soldiers lift the crosses into place one by one. We hang there with death soon due to arrive and pay its final call.

It was no accident that day that Jesus Christ hung between two thieves named Jim and Tim, for God governs the world completely. Isaiah the prophet predicted this crucifixion day around six hundred years before with these words from the book of Isa 53:12b:

> *Because he looked death in the face and didn't flinch, because he embraced the company of the lowest. He took on his own shoulders the sin of the many, he took up the cause of all the black sheep.*

WHY?

Jesus' death on the cross willingly demonstrated the depths of shame he went through for you and me to die as our substitute and pay the supreme penalty to atone for our sins.

The cross revealed what people really thought about Jesus Christ that day. And we crucify him again today if we refuse to surrender our lives to him. Jesus Christ surrendered all of heaven's glories that we might be saved for now and eternity.

Jewish leaders wanted Jesus Christ to hang on the center cross. "His life served sinners; now let him die with them."

I'm Tim, whom over the years Bible scholars came to refer to as the thief on the cross who repented of his sins. And in giving my life to Jesus Christ, I found victorious divine deliverance that day, even though I hung on a cross of death.

Your Bible records that I said to Jesus that fateful morning in Luke 23:42–43, *"'Jesus, remember me when you enter your kingdom.' He said, 'Don't worry, I will. Today you will join me in paradise.'"*

Today!

Christ's response to me brought hope in the midst of defeat, despair, and death. And if today you live without hope, having experienced life's defeats and mental despair, Jesus Christ offers the same promise to you. Christ speaks *today*.

Let me continue with my story and my message for you today.

The morning they crucified me, and Jesus Christ promised me that *today* I would be with him in heaven, began with a sentence of "guilty" pronounced by man and by God. Guilty! And the verdict was fair and correct. Before man and God, the sentence of "guilty" could not be denied.

Jim, my fellow gang member, in his death agony, hurled verbal insults at Christ.

> *"Some Messiah you are! Save yourself! Save us!"*
> *But the other one made him shut up: "Have you no fear of God? You're getting the same as him. We deserve this, but not him—he did nothing to deserve this."* (Luke 23:39–41)

Though the knowledge came late, I knew that I stood guilty before man and God.

With parched and cracked lips and a body racked with pain intensified by thirst, I looked behind at my past life judged by man and looked ahead to death that day and meeting God's judgment. The verdict remained guilty.

Remembering my past life with its errors and my sins, a ruined life, I could only think of the eternal future that offered no hope for the eternal existence of my soul. Soon I would be face-to-face with God and hear the verdict of "guilty."

How about you? If you were hanging on a cross, knowing that after a few agonizing hours you would be transported into God's presence, what would the verdict be?

Join me, a guilty thief on a cross, and cry out, "*Jesus, remember me when you enter your kingdom.*"

My one sentence expressed a marvelous statement of faith that showed faith in a second coming: "*when you enter your kingdom.*" At that moment, from my heart, my statement exceeded all normal reasoning other than faith. And as a sinner, I pleaded for Jesus Christ not to honor me but to remember me. On the brink of eternity, I realized that, even more than a desire to be taken off the cross and have my suffering eased, my greatest problem at that moment was not where I was but what I was, a hopeless person without God. My most urgent need on that day of death was salvation.

Your greatest need today is to have Jesus Christ as your Savior. You may reason that your primary need would be a change in your particular lot in life. But only Jesus Christ can change who and what you are.

On my day of death, soon to face my creator with a guilty soul, the Holy Spirit guided my consciousness and gave me at least seven simple and sound beliefs of marvelous spiritual illumination to understand what everyone bound for eternity needs to consider.

First—I believed in a future life where retribution would be handed out by a righteous and sin-avenging God. Do you?

Second—I saw my sinfulness when I said "*what our sins deserve.*" Do you?

Third—I witnessed to the innocence of Jesus Christ when I said, in Luke 23:41, "*We deserve this, but not him—he did nothing to deserve this.*" Do you recognize the purity of Jesus?

Fourth—I confessed the divinity of Jesus Christ. Do you?

Fifth—I believed in the saving power of Jesus Christ. Do you?

Sixth—I acknowledged the Lordship of Jesus: "*when you enter your kingdom.*" Do you?

Seventh—I looked forward to the second coming of Jesus Christ: *"when you enter your kingdom."* Do you?

My last words before death were confessing my guilt, as a sinner in a prayer petition to Jesus. And when Jesus gave his last promise to me before his own death, his concern was not where I was but what I was.

I, Tim, the thief on the cross, hung guilty on a cross before man and God at around 9:00 a.m. when the crucifixion began. Guilty was the verdict from man and God.

At this hour, what are YOU—guilty or forgiven?

By noon, Christ was my Savior and peace came to my troubled soul and pain-pierced body. Up to this moment in the crucifixion scene, Jesus remained silent other than to repeatedly say Luke 23:34, *"Father, forgive them; they don't know what they are doing."*

Jesus didn't respond to the crude and rude storm of insults hurled around the cross. He silently bore them when held up to contempt. But Jesus breaks the silence when a fellow sufferer on a cross, me, pleads for grace.

In the midst of that crucifixion scene, Jesus Christ's words pour forth like water flowing in a desert, in Luke 23:43—*"Don't worry, I will. Today you will join me in paradise."*

That day I found what I needed most—GRACE—not what I deserved but what I received.

My salvation refutes many ideas about how to obtain salvation today. There was no time for a religious ceremony. I was not saved by baptism—no water available. No sacraments available to be served. I was saved without church membership. I did not spend time in purgatory or a grave sleeping until the second coming of Jesus Christ. I could not offer a moral life after my conversion. I was saved without any hope of offering a lifetime of service to Jesus Christ.

Salvation came by the grace of God. Jesus said "TODAY." And today remains the sinners assurance if we place our trust in Jesus Christ.

I, Tim, the thief on the cross, became the first citizen of the new kingdom of grace. I became the first sinner to enter paradise, washed in the blood of Christ that flowed from Calvary's cross. My faith in Jesus Christ happened before many other events that would have added more strength to my petition for mercy.

I, Tim, the thief on the cross, at nine in the morning, guilty before God and man, found grace at noon—by faith.

My declaration of faith came before the hours of darkness from twelve to three; the triumphant cry by Jesus in John 19:30, *"IT IS FINISHED,"* rending of the temple veil in two; an earthquake; and the centurion's confession in Matt 27:54, *"This has to be the Son of God."*

By faith I looked to Jesus as my Savior and King, although Jesus possessed no throne but a cross, no scepter but nails in his hands, no regal wardrobe but the shame of nakedness.

Jesus Christ my King on the cross told me in Luke 23:43, *"Today you will be with me in paradise."* Jesus gave me in that simple statement at least five assurances:

1. Life goes on—paradise.

2. Abiding fellowship—with Jesus Christ.

3. A heavenly home forever.

4. An immediate heavenly home.

5. Salvation by faith finds me guilty in the morning but provides grace, so needed but in no way deserved, at noon.

Jesus Christ died at about three in the afternoon. Jim and I lived on a few more hours until the soldiers came and broke our legs to hasten death. They did not want our bodies to be on a cross during the Jewish Sabbath, which began at six. I died around five that day.

Immediately Jesus met me and personally escorted me to heaven. Angels debated as they watched the scene on earth unfold with Jesus' death that provided atonement for the sins of the world.

Who would Jesus bring first to the kingdom, since his atoning work of redemption on the cross now stood completed?

Would it be Abraham, father of the faithful, who, two thousand years before, saw Christ in his day?

Or would it be Moses, who, fourteen hundred years before, wrote about Jesus and later visited with him on the Mount of Transfiguration?

Perhaps it would be King David, whom the Bible records as a man after God's own heart.

And we must not forget Isaiah, the gospel prophet, who, six hundred years before Christ, wrote about the suffering Savior.

Would it be John the Baptist, Jesus' cousin, now dead two years, who first of all proclaimed Jesus as the Lamb of God who would take away the sin of the world?

The debate ends. Christ appears.

He brings me with him, Timothy the penitent thief, now a redeemed saint of the Lord. I stand before God the Father awaiting judgment. The Father on the throne sees me redeemed and reconciled to him through Jesus his Son, by his marvelous grace, and cries out reminding us of the prodigal son story Christ told in Luke 15:22–24:

> *Quick. Bring a clean set of clothes and dress him. Put the family ring on his finger and sandals on his feet. 23 Then get a grain-fed heifer and roast it. We're going to feast! We're going to have a wonderful time! 24 My son is here— given up for dead and now alive! Given up for lost and now found!*

I passed through death's door to instant glory forever. Believe it! God's marvelous, stupendous grace can take a person from a Roman dungeon in the morning, guilty before man and God, grant grace at noon on a cruel cross, and in the evening bring him into heaven with all of its glory. This happened all in one day!

Jesus said *today*. That day was a day of salvation for me, Tim the thief on the cross.

Today did you wake up with a load of sinful guilt, aware that if today you were to change worlds and face the Lord as your judge, you would be guilty and deserve judgment?

Today if that is so, let me share with you the wonderful truth that the grace of God stands ready and strong as it did that day when Jesus Christ gave free grace to me, a guilty sinner.

If today would be your last day on this earth, you can know the joy of heaven eternally if you have accepted Jesus Christ as your personal Savior. If Jesus can save Tim the thief on the cross, he can and will save you today.

God's word states it plainly in 2 Cor 6:2. God reminds us, *"I heard your call in the nick of time; The day you needed me, I was there to help. Well, now is the right time to listen, the day to be helped."*

You can go from guilt to grace to glory today.

Tim's Reactions

His last and only hope was Jesus Christ, and he received eternal help.

Illustrations from Personal Experience

I will share about three young people who, because of their sudden change in health, knew that death would soon come calling. Their reaction was to give their lives to Jesus Christ like the thief on the cross as a last opportunity to be ready for eternity.

The first one was a young mother with two children who moved into the area with her husband. A member of my church asked me to visit them to welcome them to the community and also invite them to our church. After a few minutes of conversation, this mother curtly stated that she had no interest in Christ or any church. Within that same year, I received a call requesting prayer for her and a pastoral visit as she had terminal cancer. Christ and the church became very important.

Another was a young man in his thirties who became an alcoholic as a teenager and continued drinking heavily until he gave his life to Christ at age thirty-three. He was determined to never start down that previous path that had led him to total dependence on his habit. He got a better paying position and enjoyed life until one fateful day. That day, he came to see me while oozing blood through his skin. Doctors said his alcoholic past had literally damaged his vital organs. He died six days later. But he had reacted earlier and turned to Jesus Christ as his savior.

Lastly, there was a young mother who wanted her small children to go to church, and she sent them, attending herself only occasionally. She had only a slight interest in church other than a place to send her children for a few hours of personal time. Then at age thirty-four she developed a brain tumor, and within a few months she died. But during her period of illness before death, she reacted and came into a right relationship with Jesus Christ.

And if today, like the thief on the cross and these others, you have reached the end of your hopes mentally, emotionally, or physically, let me recommend that you react to your current bad situation and give your life to Jesus Christ as a way to prepare for eternity.

Cecil the Centurion

Then the governor's soldiers took Jesus into the governor's residence and gathered the whole cohort around him. 28 *They stripped him and put a scarlet robe around him,* 29 *and after braiding a crown of thorns, they put it on his head. They put a staff in his right hand, and kneeling down before him, they mocked him: "Hail, king of the Jews!"* 30 *They spat on him and took the staff and struck him repeatedly on the head.* 31 *When they had mocked him, they stripped him of the robe and put his own clothes back on him. Then they led him away to crucify him.*

32 *As they were going out, they found a man from Cyrene named Simon, whom they forced to carry his cross.* 33 *They came to a place called Golgotha (which means "Place of the Skull")* 34 *and offered Jesus wine mixed with gall to drink. But after tasting it, he would not drink it.* 35 *When they had crucified him, they divided his clothes by throwing dice.* 36 *Then they sat down and kept guard over him there.* 37 *Above his head they put the charge against him, which read: "This is Jesus, the king of the Jews."* 38 *Then two outlaws were crucified with him, one on his right and one on his left.* 39 *Those who passed by defamed him, shaking their heads* 40 *and saying, "You who can destroy the temple and rebuild it in three days, save yourself! If you are God's Son, come down from the cross!"* 41 *In the same way even the chief priests—together with the experts in the law and elders—were mocking him:* 42 *"He saved others, but he cannot save himself! He is the king of Israel! If he comes down now*

from the cross, we will believe in him! 43 He trusts in God—let God, if he wants to, deliver him now because he said, 'I am God's Son'!" 44 The robbers who were crucified with him also spoke abusively to him.

45 Now from noon until three, darkness came over all the land. 46 At about three o'clock Jesus shouted with a loud voice, "Eli, Eli, lema sabachthani?" that is, "My God, my God, why have you forsaken me?" 47 When some of the bystanders heard it, they said, "This man is calling for Elijah." 48 Immediately one of them ran and got a sponge, filled it with sour wine, put it on a stick, and gave it to him to drink. 49 But the rest said, "Leave him alone! Let's see if Elijah will come to save him." 50 Then Jesus cried out again with a loud voice and gave up his spirit. 51 Just then the temple curtain was torn in two, from top to bottom. The earth shook and the rocks were split apart. 52 And tombs were opened, and the bodies of many saints who had died were raised. 53 (They came out of the tombs after his resurrection and went into the holy city and appeared to many people.) 54 Now when the centurion and those with him who were guarding Jesus saw the earthquake and what took place, they were extremely terrified and said, "Truly this one was God's Son!"

MATTHEW 27:27–54

MY NAME IS CECIL, a centurion who commanded one hundred soldiers as an officer in the Roman army.

Obviously, an obligation of my assignment for Rome involved keeping the Jews, a very proud people, under control, and that required constant vigilance. Since they believed they served a God who made them his chosen people, the idea of submission to any authority other than their Jehovah (God) often prompted rebellious responses.

However, this highly respected military position still carried some additional undesirable responsibilities, like the oversight of executions.

I dreaded this difficult task at first. As time passed, my conscience became somewhat desensitized to the violence and gore of crucifixions. I never would have lasted very long in my position if I had allowed myself to get involved the way I did one time. Let me start at the beginning of an unforgettable week in Jerusalem.

On Sunday, the first day of that week, crowded conditions prevailed in Jerusalem. The Jewish people came from near and far to worship their Jehovah in and around the temple. They intended to celebrate their deliverance from Egypt more than fourteen hundred years before with a religious ceremony they called the Passover. My men scattered about the city, listening for any signs of unrest and possible rebellion. Crowds of Jews called for careful attention on my part, so I had my men specifically patrol the temple area, where a main topic of discussion was a person called Jesus, who came from Nazareth. Very little attention did I pay to the remarks about a possible king I heard and what others reported to me. After all, could any threat come out of Nazareth, a small insignificant town located a few miles north of Jerusalem?

Then the conversation took on more meaning as people began to say that this Jesus planned to come to Jerusalem that day. But what did I care?

However, the noise grew louder around noon. People placed themselves along the main streets to see this Jesus come by. Then Jesus came riding by. I could not believe what I saw. He rode a donkey. How laughable! I am a Roman soldier; a king would never disgrace himself in such a way. Where was the stallion? A proposed king riding a donkey? Still, something was wrong with this picture, so I listened and watched the crowd more intently.

But one of the things they began to say as he approached and passed by alarmed me as a Roman officer.

> The huge crowd that had arrived for the Feast heard that Jesus was entering Jerusalem. 13 They broke off palm branches and went out to meet him. And they cheered:
> Hosanna!
> Blessed is he who comes in God's name!
> Yes! The King of Israel! (John 12:12–13)

KING! Wait a minute, only Caesar can be recognized as king. Now I knew something was definitely wrong with this!

I worked closely with the religious leaders who represented Jewish authority, so I went immediately to them and expressed my concern about this kind of language that could and would make the Roman army come down hard on them. The chief priest assured me they did not favor this religious impostor, Jesus, and would take care of the matter that week. No uprising would happen from his followers. So I waited and watched and listened.

Some of you know the rest of the story. Religious rulers called the Sanhedrin planned and plotted to destroy this new religious leader who threatened their grip of power over the people. They let me in on their plans as a political ally. They wanted me to be ready for action.

Judas, a man I knew from previous days, had become one of Jesus' followers and ended up betraying him. As a result, Judas led my men to Jesus on Thursday night of this same week, and Jesus was arrested and taken to Pilate for trial.

At the trial, they accused Jesus of treason and being a danger to the security of the Roman Empire. They told the truth, for remember I had heard the crowds clearly four days previously call Jesus the King of Israel. It was treason without a doubt. But the crowds said it, not Jesus. That charge failed.

Then the religious leaders settled on an exact charge. Jesus called himself the "Son of God," and by their Jewish law he must be executed.

Pilate expressed apprehension about the entire situation and tried to convince the Sanhedrin members of Jesus' innocence. But they would not allow it and demanded that Jesus be crucified. That was the point where Pilate finally conceded to their desires and handed this apparently innocent prisoner over to me to have him flogged and crucified.

In your outwardly contemporary civilized culture, it's hard to understand the severity of what happened to Jesus. Your culture partly romanticizes this part of Jesus' life, so you may not feel strongly moved by what happened.

Flogging required repeated lashes or blows, usually with a rod or a whip. My soldiers stripped Jesus naked and tied him to a pillar about eighteen inches in diameter with iron rings about nine feet from the ground. My soldiers hung him by the hands from those rings, so that his feet couldn't touch the ground, making it impossible for him to escape the lashes.

The whip consisted of pieces of wood, metal balls shaped like acorns, and chips of lamb bones. The pieces of bone dug into the body of Jesus, into his very muscles, tearing out chunks of flesh and exposing the bone beneath. After only a few lashes, his back and limbs were lacerated, leaving his skin in long ribbons. Victims would scream with their bodies quivering, then mercifully some would die as a result of the beating and not be crucified.

It didn't take long before Jesus became a beaten and bloody man. I stopped the flogging before he died and gave the order to my soldiers to cut his body lose from the rings that held him. He fell to the ground, his body collapsing in a pool of his own blood. My soldiers picked him up, and Jesus stood, despite the enormous loss of blood, revealing a body that vividly manifested mutilation.

What took place next fulfilled a Roman custom. When the Romans conquered a king, they would clothe him in regal robes, place him on a mock throne, and kneel before him, thus mocking his fallen status. The soldiers took the naked Jesus, placed on him a mock garment of dignity, an old cast-off cloak of mine, and made him sit on a rock in the center of the room.

Then they took some thorns about one to two inches long from a shrub called the Rhamnus, wove a crown around his head down to his ears like a hat, and struck him on the head with a reed that would drive the thorns deeper into his flesh. This caused intense pain down his face and neck.

You read in your Bible that they mocked him. The word "mocked" implies the actions of little children singing, dancing, and leaping for joy around the victim. For when the crowd said "Hail, King of the Jews!" the word "hail" means praise and glory. We degraded his body and emotions. Where is the praise and glory? To add insult to injury, we spat in his face!

Looking into Jesus' face, something happened inside of me. The way in which this man so graciously responded to this horrible torture, the way in which he looked with love at his executioners, caused me to wonder about this man called Jesus from Nazareth.

We put his clothes back on him to help soak up the blood flow from his wounds and so that the soldiers performing the actual crucifixion could share them afterwards.

To get Jesus to the site of the crucifixion, another custom needed to be observed. Crime could be deterred if the general public could see that the death sentence was actually fulfilled. Also, another custom or general rule of law made the condemned criminal carry their personal cross through the city to the place of crucifixion.

The procession began. I went first with a herald blowing a trumpet to clear the way. Another soldier walked with me, carrying the sign to be placed at the top of the cross—the title, the reason for his execution—"The King of the Jews."

The Pharisees, soldiers, leading Jews, and temple priests followed, along with the four men assigned to nail up Jesus and the other two scheduled to die on a cross. In the middle, servants carried ropes, nails, hammers, baskets, and the center pieces for the crosses.

Along the way, people lined the streets. They gawked from rooftops. Some wept. Others jeered. Whenever Jesus would fall, my soldiers would beat him and kick him until he would slowly and painfully get up and continue the march of death. The street we traveled is now called the Via Dolorosa, or the "Way of pain."

When we turned to leave the city, the road wound up a steep hill. Jesus could no longer carry his cross as shock and loss of blood drained him of nearly every last ounce of strength, and he fell, unable to stand up with his cross. My soldiers seized a man from the crowd, forcing him to carry the cross to Golgotha, the location for executions. Soldiers surrounded the hill to prevent any riots and any possibility of escape. They crucified Jesus and the two others scheduled for execution at nine in the morning.

Some people talk about hell on earth or say that war is hell. No! The closest thing to hell on earth was the death of Jesus. I just wanted the day to be over. Why, after all those years with all the executions I had carried out, did this one bother me? My head pounded. I wanted and needed to get away, but I couldn't leave—not yet—not until Jesus died.

At noon the strangest thing happened. While we were standing near the crosses, a cool breeze came through and darkness covered the sky as far as we could see. I never saw a storm forming like this one before. As the darkness moved in, I waited for the storm to hit. But nothing happened, only a strange calm that precedes storms. It lasted three long, eerie hours.

As I stood there waiting for Jesus to die, my entire life flashed before my eyes. I had worked hard to make it to this prominent position. It paid well. I felt respected; I had made a good life for myself and my family. But at what cost had I lived this way? What kind of man had I become that I could supervise the mutilation of another man and then go home and enjoy a meal with my family as if nothing had happened? I could watch nails being driven through the limbs of other human beings and then go home and kiss my children good night. What used to bother me no longer fazed me. This isn't the kind of person I wanted to be.

What had happened to me? Was I any better than the people I crucified? I knew the answer to my own question as it related to this Jesus. Something very innocent radiated from his demeanor, as I observed him. Comparing my guilt to his, even though I had the law on my side, I should be the one hanging there, not him. Yet there Jesus hung! He breathed his last breath. *Finally this would all be over,* I thought. Just then the ground began to shake beneath us. Minor tremors happened in this area but not like this one! Rocks split in two with the explosion of a mighty earthquake!

Could it be a coincidence that it happened at the very moment that Jesus died? I didn't think so! This man wasn't guilty of a crime! What he had claimed was true! He was the Son of God! I realized that I wasn't just thinking those words. I had spoken them out loud, loud enough that all those around me could hear.

Call it insubordination and contradicting my superiors, but I didn't care! The evidence overwhelmed me. God spoke to me and said this Jesus was his Son.

Then it hit me. What had I done? I had killed him! Terrified, I expected a lightning bolt to strike me dead on the spot. How angry God must be with me.

I returned home. I thought maybe if I stayed out of sight I would be safe. But everywhere I tried to hide, God could see me there—even in the darkest corners of my house. There was no place to escape from him.

Saturday, the day after Jesus' crucifixion, seemed to drag on for an eternity. I couldn't sleep. I couldn't eat. Occasionally, I had to stop myself from shaking in fear. I didn't even want to go outside but was forced to when one of my soldiers hurried in, visibly shaken. "Come to the graveyard Sir. Something you need to see."

When I arrived, some of my soldiers surrounded the place, all of them trembling as much as I had the night before. The doors of tombs stood open. Former corpses now stood alive in the graveyard, seeming to wait for something to happen. I didn't want to stay around to find out, so I left some of my men to stand guard and notify me should they try to advance outside the graveyard. Meanwhile, other work remained to do.

The Jews expressed fear that some of Jesus' followers might try to steal Jesus' body and claim he rose from the dead on the third day. They convinced Pilate to have me place soldiers to stand by and guard the tomb. We'd guarded prisoners, but never a dead one before. I did as Pilate requested, personally selecting the men. They went and did as they were instructed—a simple enough task, or so I thought.

It was early Sunday morning when two of my men who were guarding Jesus' tomb came running to me, stuttering and making no sense at all. "Spit it out!" I said.

They said, "Sir, he's . . . he's . . . he's gone! Jesus is gone!"

"What do you mean, he's gone?"

"There was an earthquake; an angel like lightning appeared and we passed out. When we came to, his body was gone! Please don't kill us! We're not lying." Somehow I knew they were telling the truth.

Nighttime darkness came in the middle of the day, an earthquake shook, dead men walked, and then an angel appeared. Jesus' body was missing. Then it hit me. From the moment when I first looked into Jesus' face, seeing no condemnation, only compassion, through the works of nature before and after he died, I knew this was no ordinary man. This man really was who he said he was. God was speaking to me again, for in that moment I realized that he was the Son of God!

Cecil's Reactions

Cecil reacted positively when faced with obvious truth. He believed that Jesus was the Son of God. Do you acknowledge this truth or deny it?

An Illustration from Personal Experience

If you discover that your occupation is not Christ-honoring, how do you react?

Jack Craver, a devout Christian, worked as an upholsterer for a chair manufacturer. The company at the annual furniture exhibition with numerous manufacturers asked Jack to upholster a chair for display. The value of a chair can vary greatly according to the quality of the frame and fabric used. Jack followed their instructions regarding the frame and fabric for the display model.

At the exhibition, the chair was a success and the company received many orders for it. Then the company told Jack to build or direct the construction of the popular chair with one main change. He was to use a cheaper fabric than the one displayed at the exhibition.

Jack had worked for the company for over thirty years and needed his job. But he refused. They threatened to fire him unless he obeyed a command contrary to his Christian principles. He said NO! The company finally relented and allowed Jack to stay in his position until he retired. Jack reacted with integrity and the Lord honored him.

And the Lord will honor you if you react with integrity.

Saul's Story

*All this time Saul was breathing down the necks of the Master's disciples,
out for the kill. He went to the Chief Priest 2 and got arrest warrants to
take to the meeting places in Damascus so that if he found anyone there
belonging to the Way, whether men or women, he could arrest them and
bring them to Jerusalem.*

*He set off. When he got to the outskirts of Damascus, he was
suddenly dazed by a blinding flash of light. 4 As he fell to the ground, he
heard a voice: "Saul, Saul, why are you out to get me?"*

He said, "Who are you, Master?"

*I am Jesus, the One you're hunting down. 6 I want you to get up and
enter the city. In the city you'll be told what to do next."*

*His companions stood there dumbstruck—they could hear the
sound, but couldn't see anyone—8 while Saul, picking himself up off the
ground, found himself stone blind. They had to take him by the hand
and lead him into Damascus. 9 He continued blind for three days. He ate
nothing, drank nothing.*

*10 There was a disciple in Damascus by the name of Ananias. The
Master spoke to him in a vision: "Ananias."*

"Yes, Master?" he answered.

*11 "Get up and go over to Straight Avenue. Ask at the house of Judas
for a man from Tarsus. His name is Saul. He's there praying. 12 He has*

*just had a dream in which he saw a man named Ananias enter the house
and lay hands on him so he could see again."*

*13 Ananias protested, "Master, you can't be serious. Everybody's talk-
ing about this man and the terrible things he's been doing, his reign of terror
against your people in Jerusalem! 14 And now he's shown up here with
papers from the Chief Priest that give him license to do the same to us."*

*15 But the Master said, "Don't argue. Go! I have picked him as my per-
sonal representative to Gentiles and kings and Jews. 16 And now I'm about
to show him what he's in for—the hard suffering that goes with this job."*

*17 So Ananias went and found the house, placed his hands on blind
Saul, and said, "Brother Saul, the Master sent me, the same Jesus you
saw on your way here. He sent me so you could see again and be filled
with the Holy Spirit." 18 No sooner were the words out of his mouth than
something like scales fell from Saul's eyes—he could see again! He got to
his feet, was baptized, 19 and sat down with them to a hearty meal.*

ACTS 9:1–19

SAUL'S (LATER CALLED PAUL) conversion story recorded in Acts
chapter 9 bears repeating again and again. As Paul, he relates his
conversion story again in Acts chapters 22 and 26. His conversion
to a devoted follower of Jesus Christ stands out as one of the fa-
mous recorded incidents in the Bible revealing what a transformed
life can become. Listen as Saul relates his story.

∼

God allowed me to be born into a respectable family in the community of Tarsus. My parents, though Jews in a gentile city, became Roman citizens. They worshiped Jehovah while enjoying the
benefits of civil obedience to Caesar. Thus, I knew and grew up in
the best of two worlds with both religious and civil advantages.

Father and mother noticed my intellectual aptitude at an
early age. They nurtured me. They tutored me. They sent me to
the best local schools. I excelled in learning about the world and

most of all about Jehovah. Every Sabbath we went to worship. I attended the Sabbath schools for children and became well-versed in my Jewish religion and the history of my people. I read and heard about the Sanhedrin, our religious governing body. I aspired to be a part of that noble group. And I wanted to be ready when the messiah came. God called me to be a defender of our religion during these perilous times of Roman occupation.

Looking back over my life, the motives that drove me forward were acceptance and fellowship. I wanted to be accepted by my religious leaders and become one of them. And it happened.

As a teenager, my parents sent me to Jerusalem to study at the Jewish seminary. Other boys played games and partied and studied only enough to pass their courses. But I applied myself. I spent long hours pouring over the ancient manuscripts. Moses intrigued me with his account of creation and the origin of our people as God's people. Chosen we were. We were special people, no doubt about it. I loved seminary. To others it seemed boring and a waste of time. But it excited me. The message from God spoke of our people being the vessel through which salvation flowed. And in veiled words, the message spoke quietly but assuredly that the messiah would come from our people.

You may not know it, but one thing constantly plagued me. My temper flared up regularly, especially if someone challenged the truth of the holy word and the worship methods of our religion. I would strongly defend God's word and our worship of Jehovah.

I advanced rapidly through the religious chain of command. At the age of thirty, the only thing hindering me from reaching my goal as one of the seventy-member Sanhedrin related to not yet finding a wife. They required members to be married. But something else slowed my progress toward marriage. Marriage would need to wait until I had performed one last duty for my Jehovah: Stamping out Christianity.

While studying in Jerusalem for several years, I began to hear about this masterful teacher who could sway an audience with his plain and direct teachings. He told stories or parables that appealed to the people. Could he be the messiah? The crowds followed this new teacher. My teachers became alarmed because some of the things he said did not correspond with their interpretation of Holy Scripture. The Sanhedrin met often to discuss this Jesus of Nazareth. They denounced him as a heretic performing miracles and teaching through the power of Beelzebub. I listened as an observer as they debated what to do with this Jesus. His stories and actions conflicted with what I knew about Jehovah and the promised messiah.

We looked for a conquering king. This peasant could not be a king. A few sleight of hand tricks did not make him the messiah. Then, with careful planning, they had Jesus arrested, tried, and crucified. With others, I cried out at his trial, "Crucify him, crucify him." And they did crucify Jesus on Friday during the Passover Feast. I thought, *Good riddance. This will stop this so called new religious movement. Their leader dies and that ends it.*

But on the first day of the week, strange things happened. Graves opened and the dead came alive. Word began to circulate that this Jesus rose from the dead. It was just another trick of the devil. We were at war with powerful demonic forces.

My temper reached an all-time high. Fifty days went by and things seemed to be calming down. The imposter disappeared and his followers became quiet.

But after fifty days, something suddenly happened in an upper room in Jerusalem. One hundred and twenty people burst out of the room. Excitement filled the air. People praised the Lord. They proclaimed Christ to be risen. The devil really knew how to mislead people.

I saw one of them stand up to speak. I later learned it was the man they called the apostle Simon Peter. A crowd of around five thousand gathered and listened. I have to admit that he spoke powerfully and forcefully. The people when he finished yelled out, "WHAT SHALL WE DO?" He called out, "REPENT," and more than half of the people bowed down and began praying, asking God to forgive them. NOT ME! This work of the devil demanded someone to stand against it and protect our Jewish religious heritage. My temper burned within.

Working with the religious leaders I schemed and planned to put this new movement to a well-deserved death. They gave me permission to pursue and prosecute those professing to be followers of Jesus Christ. Their power gave me the right to be prosecutor and judge and the defender of Judaism.

I tracked them down relentlessly. Some were beaten. In my rage at their satanic movement, I separated parents from their children and even voted to have some of them put to death. No mercy for the pagans.

One incident slowed me temporarily. When we put Stephen on trial, his words recalled our history, but he gave a different interpretation than I knew to be true as he was stoned to death.

> As the rocks rained down, Stephen prayed, "Master Jesus, take my life." 60 Then he knelt down, praying loud enough for everyone to hear, "Master, don't blame them for this sin"—his last words. Then he died. (Acts 7:59–60)

His tender attitude and words of possible truth began to convict me. I might be wrong, but I doubted it.

With renewed vengeance, I started to Damascus with a raging disposition to capture these people of the Way and stop their rebellion. Then I could stop and get married and join the Sanhedrin. They knew they could count on me.

The anticipated day arrived for me to travel, along with my assistants, to Damascus to arrest and bind up prisoners. But the Lord of heaven stopped my venture as this happened to me.

I started to Damascus seeing the situation clearly, but I arrived in a blinded state, as the Lord took my eyesight from me. I prayed. I really prayed. No "now I lay me down to sleep" prayers. I discovered that although I reveled in my brilliance as a scholar of Jehovah's holy word, my deductions were entirely wrong. Jesus was Lord. Jesus was the Messiah. Messiah had come, and I almost missed serving him.

After three days of blindness, Ananias came and prayed with me. I could see physically. But more importantly, I could see spiritually. All of my reasoning turned upside down. Most of what I formerly thought untrue now became true. And many of the interpretations I had formerly thought true now became untrue. I believed in Jesus Christ and dedicated my life to his service.

Paul's Reactions

He changed from a formerly sincere position of beliefs to the correct one. Are you willing to change when confronted with the idea that your former beliefs are not true?

He redirected his motivation factors to do right, not wrong. Paul's motivation to serve Christ replaced personal ambitions as first in his life.

An Illustration from Personal Experience

I knew a man named Luke. Luke was an alcoholic who mistreated his wife and children. His wife was a faithful Christian who loved the Lord and prayed for her husband to be converted. He did his best to keep her from even attending church. But she did attend, as best she could, and supported the church on a limited income and with a violent husband.

The pastor of the church would visit their home, and when Luke would see him arriving, he would go out the back door to avoid seeing the pastor.

The pastor of the church loved people and wanted to see Luke converted. One day the pastor called, hoping to see Luke. But Luke went out the back door of the small house. Then the pastor went around the house and met Luke as he came out of the back door. The pastor put his arm around Luke's shoulder and quietly said, "Luke, the Lord has something better for you than the life you are living. Give your life to Jesus Christ."

The pastor's loving approach broke Luke's heart and he began to weep. That day he accepted Jesus Christ as his personal Savior and repented of his sins. The former alcoholic became a pillar of the church for many years before his death.

Reacting to Life's Situations

Jesus Christ often does the impossible and uses people for his glory that we think by our standards of judging are not good candidates for service. Too often we do not even attempt to reach some people whom we think are unreachable. When Christ calls them and forgives them, react by being supportive.

John Mark, Useful for the Lord

Paul and Barnabas stayed on in Antioch, teaching and preaching the Word of God. But they weren't alone. There were a number of teachers and preachers at that time in Antioch.

36 After a few days of this, Paul said to Barnabas, "Let's go back and visit all our friends in each of the towns where we preached the Word of God. Let's see how they're doing."

37 Barnabas wanted to take John along, the John nicknamed Mark. 38 But Paul wouldn't have him; he wasn't about to take along a quitter who, as soon as the going got tough, had jumped ship on them in Pamphylia. 39 Tempers flared, and they ended up going their separate ways: Barnabas took Mark and sailed for Cyprus; 40 Paul chose Silas and, offered up by their friends to the grace of the Master, 41 went to Syria and Cilicia to build up muscle and sinew in those congregations.

ACTS 15:35–41

LET ME INTRODUCE MYSELF. My name is John Mark. You probably do not know me by my Hebrew name, John, but by my gentile name, Mark. However, before I proceed with my personal story, let me give you some of my family's background.

My Jewish parents grew up on the island of Cypress in the Mediterranean Sea. Their tribal heritage reached back centuries to

93

Levi and included Moses and Aaron in their genealogy. My grandparents, according to the custom of that day, arranged a marriage between my father and mother.

Father was fifteen years older than my mother. I was their only child. In AD 15, Father and Mother decided to move our family to Jerusalem so their young son might have more opportunities to fulfill the duties of a Levite and be dedicated to ministry for Jehovah. My older cousin Joseph, whom you know more readily by his nickname Barnabas, became a good friend and mentor.

I admired my cousin Barnabas. In Jerusalem, with some financial help from my grandparents back in Cypress and other relatives who still lived in Jerusalem, my parents built a large inn. They dedicated it to the glory of Jehovah. The inn became a leading center in Jerusalem.

Then Father died unexpectedly. Mother continued to operate the inn and did so successfully. I faithfully helped her during those difficult days. Cousin Barnabas would come and visit with us during special feast days. It was a good time for living, other than the loss of my father.

Then we began to hear about this new religious teacher named Jesus from the tribe of Judah. How could this be? Teachers of religion should be Levites like me. But people followed him.

Mother and I went to see and listen to Jesus. When he spoke, it seemed the entire world stopped to listen. How tenderly Jesus treated the misfortunate! What power Jesus displayed! No one could successfully refute his teachings. And I saw him perform some unusual physical miracles. My mother believed Jesus was the promised messiah. And so did I.

On this particular Palm Sunday, when I was eighteen, I remembered Jesus riding down the main street right by our inn as the people shouted, "Hosanna, blessed is the King of Israel." Jesus must be the messiah. But while the people shouted praises to Jesus, the Sanhedrin, the ruling religious body, plotted to kill Jesus. They were envious of Jesus' popularity with the people and miracles they could not explain.

John Mark, Useful for the Lord

On Thursday of that same week, Jesus and his disciples came to our inn, and Mother provided a spacious upper room for them for the Passover observance. I helped serve them as requested. I wanted to be near Jesus. At this time and in my mother's house, Jesus initiated the communion service, which today you also call the Lord's Supper or the Eucharist. I was there.

Jesus then left and took his disciples to a garden to pray. I wanted to follow them, but mother said, "John—time for you to go to bed." She left me in my room. But I had to follow Jesus. I slipped out and followed Jesus and his disciples at a distance.

Then soldiers came to arrest Jesus. Judas led them to Jesus. Simon Peter tried to stop them by brandishing his sword. But Jesus stopped Simon Peter from violence. Then all the disciples fled. It seems the soldiers were arresting anyone close to Jesus. They saw me hiding behind several olive trees and started after me. Motivated by fear, I ran fast. One soldier caught up with me and grabbed my bedsheet and tore it off of me. A scared teenager can run fast when threatened. I ran all the way home to my room at the inn.

In the Gospel of Mark, I tell about Jesus' arrest and then about him being put on trial.

But between the arrest and trial, I inserted these words that some of you think do not belong there: *"A young man was following along. All he had on was a bedsheet. Some of the men grabbed him 52 but he got away, running off naked, leaving them holding the sheet"* (Mark 14:51–52). I just wanted you to know that I was there when they arrested Jesus.

And I was there the next day, Friday, when they crucified my Lord and Savior Jesus Christ. How horrible! That sight left an impression on my mind and soul that never left me until my last dying breath. That day it seemed that Satan and all his demons shouted with glee. I cried.

The Sabbath slowly passed with a hopeless, eerie silence. Mother and I suffered that day as we realized Jesus was dead. Jesus' disciples huddled in a room in the inn, fearing they might be taken out and also crucified. What happened to the messiah dream?

But the next day, Jesus rose from the dead! Victory! But later at the inn, with the disciples behind locked doors, the resurrected Jesus appeared to them. I caught a glimpse of Jesus. He could actually pass through walls and doors as a spirit, but yet he was recognizable. I was there.

During the next forty days, I was there when Jesus appeared to over five hundred at once. Then a prayer meeting started in our inn. For ten days, one hundred and twenty people prayed. Count me as one of them inside that room. Count my mother, Mary, inside that room. Count the disciples inside that room. Count Mary the mother of Jesus inside that room while Simon Peter led the prayer service. I was there.

Pentecost came. The Holy Spirit came. Nothing exactly like it before or since has happened. Simon Peter became the vocal leader for us as we followed the Lord Jesus Christ. James, the half brother of Jesus, became the presiding and organizational leader of the church. I was there at the first church conference.

As you all know, Simon preached with boldness. He did not mince words. The religious leaders did not like his preaching. They arrested Simon Peter and put him in jail. That prompted the Christians to again gather at my house for prayer. We needed Simon Peter to be delivered. And delivered he was.

The Lord sent an angel to take him out of prison and when Simon Peter knocked on our door, he had trouble getting in. That was because though we prayed for his safety we expected the worst. Later he would write about me with this tender expression at the end of his first letter recorded in the Bible.

> *The church in exile here with me—but not for a moment forgotten by God—wants to be remembered to you. Mark, who is like a son to me, says hello. 14 Give holy embraces all around! Peace to you—to all who walk in Christ's ways.*
> (1 Pet 5:13–14)

My older cousin Joseph, whom we usually call Barnabas, came to Jerusalem for the Passover and witnessed the death and resurrection of Jesus. He became a believer and prayed with us at

Pentecost. A wealthy man, Barnabas gave a lot of his fortune to help those in need.

During this time, Saul, the most feared of men, tried to destroy the infant church. You know how the Lord miraculously saved Saul (Hebrew name), and he became Paul (Greek name) and was greatly used by the Lord to start churches. Barnabas helped Paul to be accepted by the church in Jerusalem, and Paul stayed at our inn until he returned to his home town of Tarsus.

Later, when news came of a revival in Antioch, the Jerusalem church sent Barnabas to guide them. Arriving there, he sent for Paul to come from Tarsus and help him. At this point in time, Barnabas definitely led the Antioch Church.

Then they received the news about a famine in Jerusalem. Responding to the news, the new church in Antioch sent Barnabas and Paul with a love offering back to Jerusalem. Then later they went back to Antioch and I went with them.

At Antioch, the church, under the direction of the Holy Spirit, sent Barnabas and Paul out on the first missionary journey of the church to win the world for Jesus Christ. And do not forget, I went as their helper.

We left for the land where Barnabas and I came from, Cypress. Working with these two older men, I enjoyed the thrill of serving the Lord, especially among relatives and even friends from my early childhood. I was really doing the work of a Levite priest now.

But then we sailed to Perga in Pamphylia. Not as exciting and definitely more dangerous. After a few days I began to remember the family inn back in Jerusalem. Comfort called. Good food called. Mother needed me. The church back in Jerusalem needed me. What purpose did I serve by being in a strange land with many hostile people? And besides, Paul became the leader of our trip and cousin Barnabas accepted it. Paul's ideas and mine did not coincide. Night came. Paul and Barnabas slept. But I, Mark, was wide awake. I left in the middle of the night. Back to Jerusalem I hurried. Yet I dreaded to meet my mother and tell her what had happened. I somehow knew she would not approve of my deserting Paul and Barnabas. And she did not approve. But I went back to Jerusalem.

Just as that night I ran from the arresting soldiers in the garden to go home, this night I ran from my friends to go home. I made a mistake in running from duty.

Back in Jerusalem I again followed Simon Peter and listened as he told about Jesus. He gave vivid details about the looks and gestures of Jesus, which I recorded in the Gospel according to Mark. Simon Peter talked more about what Jesus did than what he taught.

I can still see Simon Peter with that rugged, worn face, weathered by the sea and sun, striding back and forth as his trumpetlike voice proclaimed the truth about Jesus Christ. Simon described Jesus as a servant yet a conqueror, but always a Savior.

Then I returned to Antioch, having made peace with the Lord and my mother. Barnabas forgave me. But Paul would not let me go with them on a second missionary trip because of how I had deserted them on the first trip. My cousin Barnabas and Paul disagreed strongly. They separated. Paul took Silas, and I went with my cousin back to Cypress for another missionary adventure. This time I stayed.

Now, I was there when the two men disagreed about me. In later reflecting on it, I could see that they were both right.

Paul was right that the mission was too important to take a chance on someone who had previously failed. Yet Barnabas was right in giving someone a second chance. I thank the Lord for that second chance to be useful in the his kingdom.

In the year AD 50, I was thirty-five years old and Simon Peter was now dead. The Holy Spirit burned on my mind and heart that I needed to write down the sermons he had preached about Jesus. And the Lord gave me—a previous failure—a second chance to write the first account of the life of Jesus Christ for the entire world to read forever.

As I traveled, I again encountered Paul and served him in his latter years of ministry. Paul forgave me and used me in his ministry. I was there at most of the main happenings relating to the life and ministry of Jesus Christ and the early church's beginnings.

I was there and saw and heard Jesus teach and heal.

I was there on Palm Sunday.

I was there at the first Lord's Supper.

I was there the night they arrested Jesus.

I was there when they crucified Jesus.

I was there with the disciples behind closed doors when the resurrected Jesus appeared to the disciples and then five hundred believers.

I was there when Jesus ascended to heaven.

I was there when the Holy Spirit came at Pentecost in my house.

I was there when Simon Peter preached at Pentecost.

I was there when Simon Peter knocked on our door after an angel led him out of prison.

I was there when the church commissioned its first missionaries.

And I was there to write the Gospel according to Mark based on Simon Peter's sermons.

I have a lot of favorite Scriptures; however, let me share a personal one. The apostle Paul writes at the end of the last letter he would write in our Bible, in 2 Tim 4:11, these words that mean so much to me: *"Luke is the only one here with me. Bring Mark with you; he'll be my right-hand man."* The Greek word translated "right-hand man" carries the meaning of being both useful and able to furnish what is needed.

Mark's Reactions

He could have been angry with Paul for not giving him a second chance. He proved his worthiness to be trusted, which took several years of living faithfully for Christ before Paul would use him again.

John Mark realized his mistake and never repeated that mistake again. Avoid repeating the same mistake again.

Reacting to Life's Situations

An Illustration Familiar to Many of You

Chuck Colson was one of the main leaders of the Nixon admin-istration. "Watergate" in the 1970s became a well-known word as the actions surrounding it brought down the Nixon presidency and Nixon was forced to resign instead of being impeached.

A number of Nixon's closest advisers, including Colson, later were tried for their actions. Some were sentenced to prison, in-cluding Colson. How would he react to going from being one of the most powerful persons in the world to now being in prison?

Colson made the decision to give his life to Jesus Christ. He wrote the best-selling book *Born Again* and founded an interna-tional prison ministry to bring relief and help to prisoners and, equally important, their families. He reacted positively to a diffi-cult situation and chose to make an eternal difference in many lives during his lifetime. Colson's legacy continues on after his death.

If you are in a difficult situation because of your decisions or the actions of others, can you see a way to use it by reacting positively for yourself, family, and others?

Moses' Mistake

LET ME INTRODUCE MYSELF. I am Moses. God led me personally to record the first five books in the Bible, Genesis, Exodus, Leviticus, Numbers, and Deuteronomy. When people in your lifetime think of me, they usually remember words like "exodus," "Red Sea," "manna from heaven," "the Ten Commandments," and, of course, "water miracles." Outstanding accomplishments by human standards of measurement can be attributed to my life of service as the Lord God Jehovah made all of them possible. Yet my lifelong dream to lead the children of Israel personally into the promised land of Canaan was not realized due to some major mistakes on my part.

Today, several thousand years later, I want to share with you those mistakes. They are an example of what not to do, if you desire the fullest of God's blessings.

Let me ask you to remember, if you have read about me in the Bible, that a large portion of my life from birth to death at one hundred and twenty is connected with water and its use.

The year I was born a command from Pharaoh, Egypt's supreme leader, went throughout the land of Egypt to cast all of the newborn Israelite boys into the river Nile to drown and become possible crocodile food. My family protected me until my presence became obvious. Then my mother and my sister Miriam put me into a small boat and watched. Pharaoh's daughter saw me crying and rescued me. She named me "Moses," which means "withdrawn from the water." I became her adopted son. History reveals that this daughter had no children, and I became possibly an heir apparent to the throne of Egypt.

This might be what the Bible refers to fifteen hundred years later:

> By faith, Moses, when grown, refused the privileges of the Egyptian royal house. 25 He chose a hard life with God's people rather than an opportunistic soft life of sin with the oppressors. 26 He valued suffering in the Messiah's camp far greater than Egyptian wealth because he was looking ahead, anticipating the payoff. (Heb 11:24–26)

My life can be thought of as existing in three main sections. From birth to age forty I lived in Egypt. From forty to eighty, after fleeing Egypt for killing an Egyptian who was mistreating an Israelite, I lived with just my immediate family in the wilderness. From eighty to my death at one hundred and twenty, I lived in the wilderness as a part of the exodus from Egypt to the promised land of Canaan. We pick up my story at age eighty leading to my mistakes.

God called me to lead the children of Israel out of Egypt to Canaan. My first assignment was to get us out of Egypt through a series of ten plagues. The first one involved water, as directed by the Lord. I was to use Aaron's rod and touch the Nile River, turning it into blood.

After the terrible ten plagues, Pharaoh let us go and we started the exodus in the middle of the night. Pharaoh changed his mind and started his pursuit of us, to bring us back to Egypt. This immediately presented two problems—Pharaoh and his army behind us, and the Red Sea ahead of us to cross without boats. God again directed me to lift Aaron's rod toward the Red Sea, and the waters separated. We crossed over on dry land, but Pharaoh's army perished when they tried to cross. The two standing walls of water that cleared a path for our safety caved in and drowned them.

Then, just three days after that tremendous victory at the Red Sea and God's mighty deliverance, we came to Marah in the hot and sandy wilderness. The water was bitter. The people murmured against me, Moses, for the first time, but not the last time.

Just three days ago they sang, rejoiced, and praised the Lord and me, now they murmured. The anthem of greatness subsided into groans and grumbling. The Lord God Jehovah gave me directions. We read about them in Exod 15:22–25

> *Moses led Israel from the Red Sea on to the Wilderness of Shur. They traveled for three days through the wilderness without finding any water. 23 They got to Marah, but they couldn't drink the water at Marah; it was bitter. That's why they called the place Marah (Bitter). 24 And the people complained to Moses, "So what are we supposed to drink?"*
>
> *25 So Moses cried out in prayer to God. God pointed him to a stick of wood. Moses threw it into the water and the water turned sweet.*

Later, during the first year of deliverance from Egypt, we camped at Rephidim and, again, found no water for approximately two million people and their livestock to drink or use. Let the Bible explain what happened as I recorded it.

> *Directed by God, the whole company of Israel moved on by stages from the Wilderness of Sin. They set camp at Rephidim. And there wasn't a drop of water for the people to drink. 2 The people took Moses to task: "Give us water to drink." But Moses said, "Why pester me? Why are you testing God?"*
>
> *3 But the people were thirsty for water there. They complained to Moses, "Why did you take us from Egypt and drag us out here with our children and animals to die of thirst?"*
>
> *4 Moses cried out in prayer to God, "What can I do with these people? Any minute now they'll kill me!"*
>
> *5 God said to Moses, "Go on out ahead of the people, taking with you some of the elders of Israel. Take the staff you used to strike the Nile. And go. 6 I'm going to be present before you there on the rock at Horeb. You are to strike the rock. Water will gush out of it and the people will drink."*
>
> *Moses did what he said, with the elders of Israel right there watching. 7 He named the place Massah (Testing-Place) and Meribah (Quarreling) because of the quarreling*

*of the Israelites and because of their testing of God when
they said, "Is God here with us, or not?" (Exod 17:1–7)*

So I did as the Lord God commanded, and water came out
of the rock in front of the elders of Israel, and all the Israelites had
enough water. Water came out not because of worship or praise of
God but at a time when the people trifled with unbelief. The water
came out as an example of God's grace and patience.

I come now to the main story about my major mistakes that
the Lord punished by not allowing me or Aaron to enter the promised land of Canaan.

Thirty-eight years had gone by since God brought water
gushing out of a rock at Massah for the use of around two million
people and their animals.

The original adults over the age of twenty who had left Egypt
had died. They had refused to enter the land of Canaan after the
first eighteen months in the wilderness because they considered
the giants of Canaan bigger and stronger than God. The children
of Israel who would finally enter the land of Canaan in two more
years were now fifty-eight and younger, except for four older adults,
Aaron, Joshua, Caleb, and me. The four of us looked forward with
anticipation to entering the promised inheritance. However, two
of us would soon be eliminated.

I was then one hundred and eighteen years old. Led by God,
the children of Israel set up camp at Kadesh for several months.
The demand on the water supply at Kadesh became too great for
two million people. Streams began to dry up and the people again
started to murmur and complain. As the water supply diminished,
the flow of murmuring rose. This was the third time they grumbled
and turned on me as God's leader over the need for water.

The children of Israel seemed oblivious to all the unwaver-
ing care of the past thirty-eight years, for their fathers and mothers and now them. Sweet water came from a piece of wood being
thrown into the bitter water, and later from a rock when struck.
And in addition, for thirty-eight years God sent around twelve
freight car loads of manna every day for food except on Friday
when God sent a double load for Friday and Saturday. Again, like

their fathers they moaned and wished they had died previously as they accused Aaron and me of maliciously trying to destroy them. And although the cloud of the Lord watched over them day and night, providing manna and water, they taunted me with the absence of figs, vineyards, and pomegranates. They longed for Egypt through stories told by their parents and their memories as small children. Aaron and I went to the Lord for help and he gave instructions about receiving water from a rock, but different than before. Before, I was to strike the rock in front of Israel's elders. This time I was to speak to the rock, not strike it, before all the children of Israel. This is how it reads in the Bible.

> *Moses took the staff away from God's presence, as commanded. 10 He and Aaron rounded up the whole congregation in front of the rock. Moses spoke: "Listen, rebels! Do we have to bring water out of this rock for you?"*
>
> *11 With that Moses raised his arm and slammed his staff against the rock—once, twice. Water poured out. Congregation and cattle drank.*
>
> *12 God said to Moses and Aaron, "Because you didn't trust me, didn't treat me with holy reverence in front of the People of Israel, you two aren't going to lead this company into the land that I am giving them."*
>
> *13 These were the Waters of Meribah (Bickering) where the People of Israel bickered with God, and he revealed himself as holy.* (Num 20:9–13)

In a few months, my brother Aaron would die. In the thirty-ninth year of the wilderness journey (known as the exodus from Egypt), one year after God pronounced judgment, he reminded me of my mistakes.

> *God said to Moses, "Climb up into the Abarim Mountains and look over at the land that I am giving to the People of Israel. 13 When you've had a good look you'll be joined to your ancestors in the grave—yes, you also along with Aaron your brother. 14 This goes back to the day when the congregation quarreled in the Wilderness of Zin and you didn't honor me in holy reverence before them in the*

matter of the waters, the Waters of Meribah (Quarreling) at Kadesh in the Wilderness of Zin." (Num 27:12–14)

Then, in three of my last addresses to the Children of Israel, I said to them this word from God. This was after months of pleading with God to change his mind about not letting me enter into the promised land.

But God was still angry with me because of you. He wouldn't listen. He said, "Enough of that. Not another word from you on this. 27 Climb to the top of Mount Pisgah and look around: look west, north, south, east. Take in the land with your own eyes. Take a good look because you're not going to cross this Jordan." (Deut 3:26–27)

But God was angry (breathing hard with displeasure) with me because of you and the things you said. He swore that I'd never cross the Jordan, never get to enter the good land that God, your God, is giving you as an inheritance. 22 This means that I am going to die here. I'm not crossing the Jordan. But you will cross; you'll possess the good land. (Deut 4:21–22)

That same day God spoke to Moses: 49 "Climb the Abarim Mountains to Mount Nebo in the land of Moab, overlooking Jericho, and view the land of Canaan that I'm giving the People of Israel to have and hold. 50 Die on the mountain that you climb and join your people in the ground, just as your brother Aaron died on Mount Hor and joined his people.

51 "This is because you broke faith with me in the company of the People of Israel at the Waters of Meribah Kadesh in the Wilderness of Zin—you didn't honor my Holy Presence in the company of the People of Israel. 52 You'll look at the land spread out before you but you won't enter it, this land that I am giving to the People of Israel." (Deut 32:48–52)

You didn't honor my Holy Presence—show me proper respect—revere me as holy—sanctified me not—dishonored me—failed to lift up my holiness—are various ways the statement could be translated.

Four hundred years later, the psalmist wrote about this happening in my life in Ps 106:32–33. *"They angered God again at Meribah Springs; this time Moses got mixed up in their evil; 33 Because they defied God yet again, Moses exploded and lost his temper."*

By just human standards of judgment you may question why God severely judged me and did not allow me to fulfill my lifelong dream to lead the children of Israel into Canaan, all because I struck the rock instead of speaking to it.

Water did come out and the need for water was met. But because God answers prayer or meets a specific need through one method does not mean he is pleased with the method or the person. God was angry with me. Approximately two million sets of eyes watched me that day when I disobeyed God and failed to exalt his holy name. Again, let the Bible explain several reasons as we read it closely.

First, I, Moses, took God's honor for myself. The big "I" in me arose. For thirty-eight years prior to God's judgment on me for striking the rock instead of speaking to it, I enjoyed or endured, according to the situation, an uninterrupted line of success. God used me to bring the proudest monarch of that time to his knees and eventual death. I led the greatest exodus of people from one land to another in history at that time. The Red Sea parted. Egypt's army drowned. Manna for food fell from heaven. Water came out of rocks and bitter ponds. Our enemies lost the battle when I raised my arms.

At that time, I sat on top of the leadership world as the spiritual leader of the people. By your type of leadership titles I was the president, prime minister, chief justice, and commander of the army all rolled into one. I was it with a capital "I." I faced no rivals nor worried about reelection. Like all leaders, at times I was the wonder and envy of others.

Let me tell you from my experiences as a leader that to stand on top untouched remains as equal a task as being the follower. Being number one, the brain can reel with self-importance and the heart can become proud. It's easier to walk in the valley of humiliation on a hidden path serving God than to stand on the mountaintop of success with the glow and glory of adulation, honor, and homage. And success touched me that day when I stood before the thirsty Israelites and declared in Num 20:10, *"Listen, rebels! Do we have to bring water out of this rock for you?"*

"WE." Wait a minute. It was not "we" who brought water out of the rock, but God. Only the creator of both rocks and water can do this.

Since the beginning of time, when any leader or leaders attempt to reduce God's position of being first in honor, they fail to demonstrate the holiness of God. Since I've been in heaven for centuries, I've noticed a few people impressed with their position of prominence. They act as if the world would cease to be worthwhile without their presence.

Spiritual success blinded my responsibility to always give God the honor and recognition as first before me. Who am I? My only claim to recognition was that God had used me as his servant. My sense of self-importance on that day, when I struck the rock instead of speaking to it as God had commanded, caused me to fail to honor the holiness of God. God brings forth water out of a rock, not Aaron and I.

Another reason God judged me quickly was my harsh reaction to the ingratitude of the people.

For thirty-eight years, the Israelites did at least two main things—they marched and they murmured. This was the third time they failed to trust God and me about the need for water, and they became an infuriating mob of people.

They broke through every barrier of appreciation, gratitude, patriotism, and respect for leadership. My self-confidence began to waver and turn to anger as they violently demanded water and stood ready to stone Aaron and me, just as their fathers had thirty-eight years before.

These thoughts rapidly raced through my mind that day. *I'm one hundred and eighteen and not only getting old—I am old. Is this the way they appreciate thirty-eight years of leadership? I could have possibly been pharaoh of Egypt, the largest and strongest nation at that time in history.* Once, I stood between them and God when he wanted to wipe them off the face of the earth; I interceded for them because I loved them. But evidently they didn't love me as they should. And their ingratitude for me created resentment that boiled over, and I angrily expressed it. I said, "YOU REBELS," and I said it harshly. I was mad. But was the holiness of God exalted with my words and my tone of speaking? No!

I remember that they deserved that tongue lashing I gave them. However, I failed to fulfill God's directions on how to bring water from the rock.

Which reminds me that I, Moses, was right and wrong at the same time. Rebels—yes! My actions and attitude—wrong.

God denied me the privilege of leading them into the promised land because I took honor for myself and Aaron rather than giving God the glory. Resentment followed, and I paid the price for my rash words and attitude.

A third reason for judgment on me that day came because I got in a hurry, acting ahead of God. Impatience uncontrolled produced a hurried response and I struck the rock rather than speaking to it as God directed.

It happened before when I killed an Egyptian for mistreating my people. It happened a second time when I came down from the mountain after meeting with God and receiving the Ten Commandments on stone as God made them. And seeing a golden calf, I lost my patience with my people and broke the Ten Commandments. Then I had to replace them and carve them on tablets of stone by hand, which was a hard and difficult task. I learned the hard way when I attempted to do something, even if needed and right for God. But when I did it my way instead of waiting on God, I failed to exalt his holiness.

And God punished me because, in my anger, I used rash words. A time for anger exists, but only when directed by God.

When impatience ran deep and imagination ran high, angry speech gushed out and I failed to exalt God's holiness,

The psalmist approximately four hundred years later said it very bluntly in Ps 106:32—"*And rash words came from Moses' lips.*"

My prayer for you today as you read about my mistakes is that God daily will enable you to speak to the right issue, at the right time, with the right words, and with a right attitude. When right, we can afford to keep our temper. If wrong, we cannot afford to lose it.

God's judgment on Aaron and me that day occurred when my bad attitude led to a wrong action. I struck the rock twice instead of speaking to it. The apostle Paul fifteen hundred years later told everyone more about the meaning of the rock.

> *Remember our history, friends, and be warned. All our ancestors were led by the providential Cloud and taken miraculously through the sea. 2 They went through the waters, in a baptism like ours, as Moses led them from enslaving death to salvation life. 3 They all ate and drank identical food and drink, meals provided daily by God. 4 They drank from the Rock, God's fountain for them that stayed with them wherever they were. And the Rock was Christ.* (1 Cor 10:1–4)

> *God said to Moses and Aaron, "Because you didn't trust me, didn't treat me with holy reverence in front of the People of Israel, you two aren't going to lead this company into the land that I am giving them."* (Num 20:12)

My main purpose in life was more than leading Israel to and into the promised land of Canaan. In my life and in your life a paramount purpose is to glorify, honor, and be an example of the holiness of God.

These summarize my mistakes. When spiritual success causes us to think we perform miracles and take the honor for ourselves; when the ingratitude of others comes (and it will at times) and creates resentment; when we become impatient and get ahead of God; when rash words fall from our lips; and when we take foolish action the holiness of God is not exalted.

Moses' Reactions

Observing Moses' responses, let me encourage you to remember that life's tests are there to make us not break us.

God did not permit Moses to enter Canaan with Israel at that time, which was a major disappointment to Moses. However, during the time of Christ around fourteen hundred years later, he got to come to Canaan and meet Jesus Christ on the Mount of Transfiguration. Despite Moses' mistakes, God forgave him and took him to heaven.

If you make mistakes that take you out of God's will for your life, know that God still loves you and imparts grace for your life when you ask for forgiveness. Depend on God's help to put your life's mistakes behind you.

An Illustration from Personal Experience

Sometimes God's will, which we believe and personally desire for our life, changes unexpectedly. And while our original response to God's call for service still stands, it may take a different route to discover and experience its fulfillment.

In my congregation, I became acquainted with a lady, then in her early sixties, who was bubbling with energy in service for Jesus Christ and his church. Observe how she reacted to a life situation that at first seemed contrary to God's will.

She grew up in a loving, Christian home. Giving her life to Jesus Christ as a teen, her priority in life was to serve Jesus Christ. Then Christ used her gift as an exceptional pianist in missions and church services and led her to be a missionary in South America and eventually meet the right man to marry and raise a family. She prepared for Christian service by graduating from college and seminary ready for overseas service as a missionary.

She went to South America, and God honored her work. While there, she met the man of her dreams, fell in love, and planned to marry. Then things unexpectedly and quickly changed. After being on the mission field for several years and before marriage, she had to return home due to family needs. Her missionary tenure overseas eventually ended as well as her marriage plans. Then she gradually lost the flexibility of her hands due to a genetic condition and had to give up her dedication to playing the piano for church. Three dreams of being a missionary, a wife, and a musician seemingly died. Had God misinformed her, or had she missed clear directions from the Lord? What was left of her original desires and calls to service for Jesus Christ? From what I know, her reactions to these setbacks included several things.

Back home, she served the Lord by helping start several new churches. Teaching Spanish as a high school teacher, she served as an informal missionary for Christ to the students. Even though more than twenty years have passed since her retirement, a number of her former high school students still come to see her and remember with appreciation her sincere Christian witness and her kindnesses to them.

In her immediate, somewhat isolated neighborhood of about twenty homes, she and two other ladies do missionary work. When a need arises, they meet that need if at all possible. They provide food, mow lawns, take care of pets, counsel, and work with children when needed. They live in a mission field in America.

For a number of years, they hosted a regular Friday night dinner for the community, with as many as twenty attending, to have fellowship and fun and to share Christ with them.

She reacted to disappointment in love, overseas missionary service, and the loss of a musical gift by remaining a Christian missionary. God called her, and he has confirmed that call over the years. It has been and is a life well lived in spite of unexpected setbacks.

We can ask ourselves the question pertaining to much of our lives: am I, are you, reacting to your current life situation with a continued faith that God knows best, even when disappointments and setbacks to our plans occur as we seek to ascertain and to obey God's will for our lives?

An avenue to being at our best in life is controlling our reactions positively as much as possible and glorifying God while finding peace for ourselves in the process.

John the Beloved Apostle

It was about that time that the mother of the Zebedee brothers came with her two sons and knelt before Jesus with a request.

21 "What do you want?" Jesus asked.

She said, "Give your word that these two sons of mine will be awarded the highest places of honor in your kingdom, one at your right hand, one at your left hand."

22 Jesus responded, "You have no idea what you're asking." And he said to James and John, "Are you capable of drinking the cup that I'm about to drink?"

They said, "Sure, why not?"

23 Jesus said, "Come to think of it, you are going to drink my cup. But as to awarding places of honor, that's not my business. My Father is taking care of that."

MATTHEW 20:20–23

A revealing of Jesus, the Messiah. God gave it to make plain to his servants what is about to happen. He published and delivered it by Angel to his servant John. 2 And John told everything he saw: God's Word—the witness of Jesus Christ!

*3 How blessed the reader! How blessed the hearers and keepers of
these oracle words, all the words written in this book!*
Time is just about up.

REVELATION 1:1–3

I AM JOHN, AN apostle of Jesus Christ. He asked me to share the
story of my life. When you read the story of Jesus' life as recorded
in the Gospel bearing my name, John, you may notice that I omit-
ted the time when my mother, my brother, James, and I asked a
special favor of Jesus. We wanted to be just below Christ, in authority in a new government. Now I am ashamed of our actions
recorded both in Matthew's Gospel (20:20–25) and Mark's Gospel
(10:35–40). I want to share my reaction to being disappointed and
my dream at that time in history, a vision for the future.

You already know my name is John. My father was Zebedee
and my mother was Salome. I also had a brother—James. My father had a prosperous fishing business, one that he trained James
and me to manage one day in the future, to continue his legacy.

Our family was active in the synagogue in Jerusalem, yet I
still found time to get into trouble occasionally. Sound familiar?
People who knew me described me as being intolerant, ambitious,
trustworthy, and humble. You heard me right—the last two traits
don't fit the first two. The last two, trustworthy and humble, only
became true, however, when I started serving with my cousin Jesus! Yes, the Jesus you worship.

Prior to following Jesus, my ambition was to become a leader
of our community as the best and most successful business man
possible. I wanted to be out front garnering the respect and ad-
miration of others. That early ambition carried on into my initial
phase of ministry. My brother, James, and I shared similar values
and visions. My father set an example of leadership that was also
encouraged by our mother, who wanted, with good intentions, for
her sons to succeed in life.

When I told my father that I would not be a fisherman but
instead be like Jesus, a fisher of men with my brother, James, he

was disappointed. However, he willingly gave us our freedom to pursue Christ's call for service. James and I left on our new journey of life with Christ.

What I saw and experienced in those three years of travels with Jesus will astound you.

You are quite impressed with all the innovations and discoveries that relate to medicine in your century. Miracle drugs wipe out many diseases or cure them. You have robotic surgery, heart and other organ transplants, artificial limbs that function as well or almost better than the ones that God gave you. Why, you can even have a doctor visit over a TV screen. All of that is good in your culture and time, but does it equal what happened in my day, and not just in the medical field?

My visions/dreams were right in front of me—real time. How about these on-the-spot events? The blind could see again. The lame could walk again. Lepers were cleansed and permanently cured. Thousands were fed with only a few fish and loaves of bread. Dead people came back to life. Demons were driven out of people and lands. Jesus walked on water and stilled raging storms. He was crucified but rose again on the third day. Thousands saw him after his death. Do you not see that all of your modern "miracles," though wonderful, cannot compare to what Jesus did then and will do one day? It didn't take research and millions of dollars. It was instantaneous.

Our Jewish history led many scholars to believe that a king would come forth, gather an army together, and defeat even the great Roman Empire with its military might. For that to occur, we would need an outstanding leader for the people to follow. And we would also need a supply chain of food and other supplies. With Jesus leading the way with his miraculous power to feed thousands with just a few pieces of bread and fish, how could we fail? But this goal to be in high authority had to do with my earthly life. That dream for a deliverance from Rome's oppression died with Jesus' death. Or did it die?

It's painful to tell you what you already know about our last Passover meal with Jesus and his crucifixion the next day after a mock trial. However, these events inspired me to continue where he left off—preaching against religious and political injustices and calling sinners to repentance. Not surprisingly, I was arrested too, but God spared me the excruciating death on a cross. I can even say that I was glad that I was not imprisoned in the traditional sense. Instead, I was exiled to the isle of Patmos. This miracle happened as predicted by Jesus—I would be the last original disciple of Jesus to die, in my nineties.

Before I continue with my life story as it ended on the isle of Patmos, and where Christ himself gave me a revelation of future events, recall that God often did this throughout the Bible. However, since skeptics may scoff at my story of future sights and changes to come, culminating in Christ's return, let me remind you who live in the twenty-first century that what was once science fiction has happened. You are no longer amazed with what was once the bizarre or unthinkable.

Go with me back in time to when science fiction portrayed objects flying in the air; lights burning at night without kerosene; people communicating with one another though separated by many miles; riding carts moving without being horse-drawn; and travel to planets in outer space.

Today we can say, because we experience these things, "What's so strange about airplanes, electricity, television, cars, and traveling to the moon?" That's the whole point of telling you these things. To you, they aren't strange; they are commonplace, including all the other everyday things that were once thought strange but are now familiar. Some of what we called science fiction years ago is now fact.

What about the dreams and visions in my day, the early New Testament days? Were my contemporaries astounded? How did they react to what we now call prophesies that were revealed through dreams and visions?

Here's my observation of events so far, both from ancient times through these modern times. Everything God revealed from the garden of Eden up until now by way of things to come has been verified by history as fact. Actually, our Bible is the only prophetic book whose prophecies have all come true so far. What about the future? What about eternity?

Look around you! Atrocities are being committed all over the world. Starvation and sickness run rampant, even in some developed countries. Very little respect for life in any form exists. Unusual weather patterns bring mass destruction in places that had never experienced them before. Where is God? Does he see all this? Does he have anything to say about when and if it will end? YES! That is why God allowed me to be sent to the isle of Patmos in exile.

Patmos is where Jesus revealed to me in a series of visions the future of our world and the fulfillment of eternity. What did Jesus say to me? For that, you will have to read the last book in the Bible, Revelation. God said that anyone who reads it will be blessed. That should be an extra incentive. Because the visions are so graphic and may be disturbing, I strongly suggest you have a teacher or pastor guide you through its predictions. If you are a believer, you will find the greatest comfort in knowing that one day injustices and suffering will end. If you are not a believer, I pray you will see the truth in all that I have said. Especially remember what I said about the Bible. It is the only prophetic book whose prophecies have historically come true 100 percent so far. Are you willing to risk believing that Revelation's predictions are not true? You are much braver than I could ever be!

John's Reactions

After the authorities arrested Jesus, John remained close by while the other disciples fled into the night. None of the disciples besides for John are recorded as watching Jesus die on the cross the next day. John stood at the foot of Jesus' cross and at Jesus' request promised to look after Mary, the mother of Jesus, from that day forward.

That reaction says that even when situations are at their darkest, a real friend reacts by doing all he can, even if it only means standing by to lend support.

John reacted positively to his disappointment of not being a ruler on earth with Christ when Christ died on the cross. John continued to serve, and Christ used him to write five books of the Bible (a gospel account of Jesus' life, three letters, and Revelation).

An Illustration from Personal Experience

A mentor of mine, Dr. Roy S. Nicholson, strongly impressed on me as a ministerial student the importance of the Bible as God's word and why we should believe it and respect it. I was there when the following took place.

On Tuesday at one o'clock, ministerial students attended a weekly homiletics class taught by Dr. Nicholson. One day he came in, and from his general demeanor it was obvious he was very upset. In his right hand was an empty bottle of soda. What had happened?

On his way to the class, Dr. Nicholson observed this soda bottle sitting on a Bible. That day, he lectured emphatically for forty-five minutes, not on homiletics but on the sanctity of the Bible as God's word. No one admitted to laying a soda bottle on the Bible and obviously kept quiet. As a personal conviction of mine, even to this day, when I see any object on a Bible I immediately remove it.

Do you, do I, believe and respect the authority of God's word—our Bible? The answer for me is a "yes."

Conclusion

WE ARE OFTEN NOT responsible for the circumstances we find ourselves in, but we are answerable for the way we allow those conditions to affect us. We can either let them defeat us, or we can permit them to change us into what God wants us to be. It is the author's prayerful desire that your daily reactions to life's situations, whether they are small, large, or difficult ones, will be based as much as you can ascertain on your love for and commitment to the Lord Jesus Christ and the principles of guidance found in the Holy Bible.

www.ingramcontent.com/pod-product-compliance
Lightning Source LLC
Chambersburg PA
CBHW060402090426
42734CB00011B/2230